RAVIOLI RULES

A MANAGER'S GUIDE
TO GET THE WORKPLACE COOKING

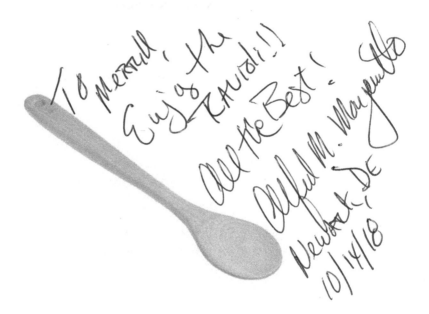

ALFRED M. MANGANIELLO, MPA

Dedication

Dedicated to my Grandparents and Parents
who showed me how to make the Ravioli.

Published by TS Publishing
116 West Gay Street
West Chester, PA 19380

Manufactured in the United States of America

Book Production by Mary Jo Casey and Dan Harvey
Website Design by TSP Chris Cotter and Joe Acchione
Logo Designed by Valerie Briglia

The events depicted in this book are fictitious.
Any similarity to any person living or dead is merely coincidental

Address comments and questions to Al Manganiello
by emailing: Ravioli@RavioliRules.com

RAVIOLIRULES.COM

Contents

Introduction

Ravioli Rules: A Manager's Guide to Get the Workplace Cooking is a story about learning, listening, growing and doing the right thing.

The book's characters learn and evolve. They reflect on a lifetime's experience, just as we develop personally, professionally, socially and spiritually. The work is about doing better today than yesterday, and doing better tomorrow than today – it's even about doing better in the afternoon than we did in the morning.

Let me tell you how this book came about.

The story and its themes result from my own growth and development, and a long-term life education. It encompasses my life experiences, and the subsequent knowledge gained through these experiences, as well as readings. All represent different points in my life. All helped me evolve, and they culminate in this story.

More than that, I see this work as the realization of an opportunity – to share management skills and lessons, and to leave behind sound advice based upon my experience.

For my story, Ravioli is a key ingredient – a metaphor, a symbol. When I was a young boy, I'd visit my grandparents on holidays. I recall the freshly made Ravioli laying out on the beds, covered with a damp cloth to keep it from drying out. When I later related the memory to my daughters, they asked me why on a bed. My grandparents lived in a tiny apartment, I explained; there was no kitchen counter space. Perhaps that's why I looked at these Ravioli in awe. Indeed, even at my young age, I perceived the planning, preparation and work that went into their making. At the time, Ravioli was merely part of a holiday meal. But many years later, my vivid memory became the spark of a management book.

In college, I majored in political science and thought I would attend graduate school for the same subject. However, my first public administration class changed my life's direction. I was a young, eager college student and enjoyed the class so much that I decided to pursue a master's degree. I liked the idea of managing in the public sector. The first person I should thank is my college professor, the late Richard Biondi, who held a Master's Degree in Public Administration and provided me my introduction. I enjoyed his theoretical classes and the subsequent internships, where I put knowledge to practical use – education through experience. I always preferred the practical over the theoretical, and that's why this management book is more than an academic text.

It's about analogy. And so I also need to thank my college fraternity brother John Perone, who pointed out that I always made food analogies when it came to learning, life, goal searching and dreams. It took me a long time to realize these food analogies served a purpose.

My graduate education in public administration supplemented my undergraduate learning. I was fascinated by management theory, as well as how people behave and what motivates them. I was inspired by great teachers, including Drs. Chris McKenna, Robert Muzenrider, as well as Dennis Butler and the late Dr. Rupe Chislom. Further, my education was supplemented by publications such as the Harvard Business Review and Public Administration Review, which coupled case studies with articles about management theory and understanding human behavior.

Graduate school required an internship, and I chose mine in the legislature. This led to a 10-year profession. The experience was perfect for someone educated in political science and public administration. I had the best of two worlds; I learned about the politics of the legislature and legislative administration. During an alumni weekend, one of my undergraduate professors told me that I was one of few political science majors employed in my field of education.

That legislative career led me into executive administration, working eight years in the government. My manager, Connie Foster, led by example: She was innovative and pragmatic and always wanted to do the right thing. She left behind her a positive legacy. I was always grateful for her excerpts from the book "The Leadership Lessons from Attila the Hun" she included on her weekly department summaries to the entire senior staff. During this period, I supplemented my management skills by reading works such as "In Search of Excellence" and "A Passion for Excellence," as well as by engaging in exercises during management retreats. I also educated myself on the Malcolm Baldridge Quality Award principles and criteria.

After my 8 years in state government executive administration ended, I transitioned to the private sector. For 12 years, I worked for a credit card company and assumed a variety of progressive management roles, including several in Corporate Quality Assurance. This expanded opportunity enabled me to sharpen my skills in areas related to management practice and philosophy.

Meanwhile, I continued reading books such as "Built to Last," "The Power of Nice," "Born to Win," "It is Never Too Late to Start," "Ground Rules for Winners," "Fighting for Life" and "Eyewitness to Power." One thing I realized: Continual education, even if it is personal and informal, is motivation's cornerstone. It keeps people fresh and energized. In my own case, I was inspired by the aforementioned works, and I perceived how the message could be translated into practical application.

I was encouraged to take the Dale Carnegie class and enjoyed the program and its two books, "The Dale Carnegie Scrapbook" and "Pathway to Success." This led me to set a new goal: to write a novel. That ambition led to this book.

Two more books inspired me: "Cigars, Whiskey and Winning: Leadership Lessons from Ulysses S. Grant" by Al Kaltman and "Who Moved My Cheese?" by Spencer Johnson, MD. The first is an interesting merger of two subjects I enjoy – history and executive decision making. The combination resulted in a unique book that addressed judgments and decisions, and it was filled with common sense. The second book resonated very strongly with me (except that I was thinking more about moving the cannoli). It sparked an idea.

I remembered my friend John Perone's remark about my analogies to food. Then, I watched a Food Network show that revealed how meal preparation—with all of its necessary skills, planning, organization and timing—was essentially project management. I thought of the Ravioli laying on the bed in my grandparents' house, and I decided to write about Ravioli.

I consulted with management and education colleagues and friends about this Ravioli/management concept. Did it make sense, I asked them. Over lunch, I ran the idea by Bob Turner (and, no, we did not eat Ravioli), and he said he could see himself teaching a course based on the concept. Another friend, author Ken Wolensky, who wrote "The Life of Pennsylvania Governor George M. Leader: Challenging Complacency" and co-wrote "Knox Mine Disaster: The Final Years of the Northern Anthracite Industry and the Effort to Rebuild a Regional Economy," remarked that I was on to something. That encouraged me. Further inspiration came from two of my managers, Bill Kleman and Jinine Martin, as well as other friends who had published their own books: Dr. Michael Powers, "Icons" and "Acts of God and Man: Ruminations on Risk and Insurance;" Bob Krouchick "47 Days That Changed America;" Vince Carocci "A Capitol Journey: Reflections on the Press, Politics, and the Making of Public Policy in Pennsylvania;" Former State Senator Franklin L. Kury, "Clean Politics, Clean Streams: A Legislative Autobiography and Reflections;" John McKenney, "Dart;" and Jamie Kleman, "It's Not Mean to be Green."

Finally, I would like to thank Mary Jo Casey (Joey), who served as overall project manager and directed the editing and publishing of Ravioli Rules. Her experience, dedication, guidance and cooking skills took this book from the shelf to the table. I listened to her advice and counsel. In particular, the sketches in this book were not only her idea, but an original design from her kitchen table when she made Ravioli. The cover of the book is her homemade Ravioli. Thank you, Joey!!!! I would thank Dan Harvey, for editing the book. Also, thanks to Chris Cotter and Joe Acchione who designed the Web site and Valerie Briglia, who designed the logo. Thank you all for your managerial cooking skills to present the Ravioli on the table for others to enjoy!

My narrative involves two cousins, Abigail and Theresa, who are trying to eat the Ravioli at a Sunday family dinner. But they're denied, and this initiates a series of events. Their grandfathers, Alfredo and Mario, share a similar experience that happened when they were young. The grandfathers teach Abigail and Theresa the Ravioli Rules, which they learned over time. Abigail and Theresa intently listen through this story, absorbing the details. Alfredo and Mario meet with many people throughout this journey, but they are the main characters, telling a story and sharing all the lessons learned from their experiences. By the end, Abigail and Theresa, after listening to the story, offer a new perspective on the Ravioli Rules.

Think of the Ravioli Rules as a big Ravioli buffet, with different types of the best Ravioli for you to pick and choose. You could try them today and choose to eat it today or decide not to eat it until later. This is a buffet that never closes. You can use any of the Ravioli Rules at any time.

So, now we are all here. The table is set.

Enjoy the Ravioli!

RAVIOLI - THE BEGINNING

Twin brothers Alfredo and Mario are now in their 60s and celebrating life. They share a memory of a family Sunday dinner – a Ravioli day. The family gathers in the combined kitchen/dining room, anxiously awaiting the Ravioli that will be served in a large, round, colorful pasta dish.

Alfredo and Mario's 10-year-old granddaughters Abigail and Theresa—cousins born four months apart—were upstairs getting cleaned and dressed after playing soccer all day. When they came downstairs, they were ready to eat some Ravioli.

The girls were tired, and as the family started serving the Ravioli, they fell asleep on the living room couch. Alfredo and Mario watched as their granddaughters dozed off. After sleeping for three hours, the girls were awakened by the noise of the dinner cleanup. They rushed to the dinner table, looking for the big Ravioli-filled dish. But it was gone.

They checked other dishes for the beloved Ravioli. No luck. They ran into the kitchen. There wasn't even any Ravioli in the refrigerator. Even the back room, where food was prepared, was empty of Ravioli. The inventory was gone. The girls panicked. They ran into the dining room and cried that the Ravioli was gone. "Who took our Ravioli? No one thought of us! We're family, too!" Alfredo and Mario watch the scene unfold. Should they counsel the girls, they wonder; or should they let Abigail and Theresa learn on their own? Should they share their own similar experience?

They picked up the girls and sat them on their laps. "We have a story for you," Alfredo said. "What is it Gramps?" Abigail said, tears still misting in her eyes. "When my brother and I were your age we, too, experienced losing our Ravioli." Theresa looked up at grandfather Mario. "You, too! Who took your Ravioli? Tell us what happened!"

It was also on a Sunday, Mario began. "And the event changed our lives forever, and for the better. It was a great learning experience, girls, and all about Ravioli. It has to do with getting, looking at, experiencing, making and presenting the Ravioli," he related. "Making the Ravioli involves a lot of practical experience that we can all learn. Ravioli is something you want to achieve, a goal to reach. Sometimes, it could be used as an example of how to treat other people, how to get things done, how to manage a project, sometimes it is even used as a guide for how to get you through life."

"The story begins many years ago, when we were little kids, just like you," adds Alfredo.

FIFTY YEARS EARLIER: RAVIOLI – THE DISCOVERY

It's another family dinner Sunday. About 35 people arrive for this food celebration – including Uncle Vito, Aunt Marie, Uncle Antonio and his wife and family. For this day, Ravioli was the special pasta. Homemade early in the morning, the Ravioli was spread throughout the house – on the kitchen table, on counters, on basement tables and even spread on the beds, including Alfredo's and Mario's. All Ravioli were covered with a damp towel or table-cloth, to keep the fresh pasta from drying out. Alfredo and Mario watched their mother boil four huge pots of water. "Mom, mom! Will there be enough for us?" exclaimed Alfredo and Mario, almost in unison. "Don't worry, my little boys, I have plenty of pasta," their mother soothed. "But if we run out, I will have saved a special Ravioli dish for both of you. I will keep it in the refrigerator."

Little Mario and Alfredo beamed at their mother's thoughtfulness – imagine, saving a dish just for them! As the Ravioli weren't served yet, Alfredo and Mario decided to take a brief nap in their rooms, as they were tired from playing soccer. Fortunately, the Ravioli that had been placed on their beds had been the first removed.

The boys' 10-minute nap turned into a three-hour sleep that lasted through the family dinner. Alfredo was the first to awake. "The Ravioli!" he exclaimed. Mario opened his eyes. "Let's get down to the dining room!"

But there was no Ravioli on the table. Alfredo and Mario looked at each other, sharing the same fear. Are there no Ravioli? They searched, but could find none. Then they remembered: Their mom had promised to save some Ravioli for them in the refrigerator. They rushed to the "fridge" and searched each shelf, knocking over food dishes (and even the dessert) to find where their mom hid their Ravioli.

Alarmed by the noisy activity, their mother came into the kitchen. She helped them in their search. But she could find no Ravioli, either. "I know I left them in here," she said, befuddled. She pulled everything out of the re-frigerator, but still she couldn't find any Ravioli. Alfredo and Mario were frustrated, whining, even mad at their mom.

Uncle Vito came into the kitchen to say goodbye and thank his sister for the great Ravioli. "They were so good that I wanted more, and I found two plates just for me in the refrigerator," he enthused. "I could not resist. I enjoyed them in the backyard with a glass of wine."

"Uncle Vito, you ate our Ravioli," the boys cried. "What right did you have? The plates had our names on them!" Uncle Vito made a quick getaway. The boys shouted behind him. "Go eat Ravioli in your own house, don't come back here again," said Alfredo. "Wait until we come to your house and eat your favorite things," threatened Mario.

The boys were still crying when their mom put them to bed. She tried to calm them down. "It will all work out." "We never want to see Uncle Vito again," said Alfredo. "He hurt our feelings, and we don't like him, either," complained Mario. "We would not do this to him," added Alfredo. "He doesn't care about us. We won't ever go to his house." "Oh, now," said their mom. "I am sure you will want to go to his house." "No," cried Alfredo. "We never want to see him again." "He hurt us," said Mario.

The following week, Uncle Vito came to visit and brought gelato. When the boys saw him coming, they ran past their mom and went outside to play with friends. They were so quick, their mom couldn't stop them, which dismayed her. She and Uncle Vito had planned this meeting to help the boys get over their hurt feelings and forget the Ravioli episode. But the boys had no interest in being part of the family.

A few days later, Alfredo and Mario reflected on their lost Ravioli. Reasoned thought replaced hysteria. They were no longer so quick to lay blame. The reflection revealed their emerging maturity, which was already well beyond their years. This proved a turning point in their young lives.

"You know, I'm not sure if that was Uncle Vito's fault," said Alfredo. "I know," agreed Mario, "After all, we went to sleep. If we stayed awake, we would have had our—I mean—the Ravioli like everyone else." "I feel like we were responsible as well," said Alfredo. "Even though there was a dish in the fridge, we should not always rely on the dish being there. It really didn't have our names on it." "Yeah, its' not like somebody took our Ravioli," said Mario. "It wasn't our Ravioli anyway. It was everybody's. We missed our opportunity because we slept. It could have been ours, but we missed it. We can't let that happen again."

Alfredo considered his brother's words. "We blamed Uncle Vito when it was really our responsibility." In his youthful way, he realized that their failure to stay awake amounted to a failure to act. "We thought we were entitled. We were selfish to believe it was just 'our' Ravioli, and because we didn't act, we blamed Uncle Vito. We were just as selfish as he was." Alfredo realized their expectation was the Ravioli would always be available, or that someone would think of them and share. "We are the only ones responsible," he observed. "We never realized we were not entitled to the Ravioli," said Mario.

Their reflection led to some solutions. The boys realized that they shouldn't panic and overreact if they failed to get the Ravioli the first time. They realized the value of patience and persistence, and they'd recover from the missed Ravioli. "We'll just work harder, listen intently, and watch and act for the next opportunity to get the Ravioli," said Alfredo. "We need to put plans in action to make sure we get the Ravioli next time," agreed Mario.

Alfredo started thinking out loud. "We can push Uncle Vito out of the way or someone can distract him so we can take the Ravioli that he would eat." "No," said Mario, "that wouldn't be right. When we are around the table, in line for the Ravioli, we need to act like gentleman, as adults. We can be aggressive, but let's not take too much that we offend others. We can't be obnoxious." It was dawning on Mario that the people at the Sunday dinner are relatives, and the way the boys behave and the image they convey will affect how these family members treat them in the future. "We can't sit eating Ravioli at the table of ladies and gentlemen if we don't behave as gentlemen ourselves." "You're right," said Alfredo. "I never thought of it. Imagine if we misbehave or are troublemakers. We will never be invited into someone's house for Ravioli. We need to be nice and work with people to build relationships, so we can enjoy future Ravioli." "Being nice with people, to make and get the Ravioli, will come in handy in the future," decided Mario.

Alfredo and Mario didn't realize it, but they were starting to learn how to build relationships. In two weeks, they were going to Aunt Caterina's house for Sunday's pasta day. So they put a plan in place that allowed them to stay awake during the Ravioli presentation and serving. They were not going to lose out again. This time they would ask the time of the serving and the details about the serving. "Will it be buffet or sit-dinner family style?"

When they learned it was buffet, they asked where the line started. This information provided them with more knowledge than anyone else and allowed them to position themselves to be first in line. Then they thought of something else: What if there isn't enough Ravioli for people last in line? Instead of just thinking about themselves, they'd share their Ravioli – a decision based on their recent experience, and a token of good will. If some people missed the Ravioli because they were late, sharing would be better than being selfish – like Uncle Vito.

"We should remember how we felt and learn from it," said Alfredo. "We should always learn from other people's behavior, good or bad, and model ourselves to be the best." So, they'd share – especially with children who are new to Ravioli and want more. And they'd watch others as they were getting the Ravioli. They'd model themselves after those demonstrating better behavior, learning from the best.

At the dinner, little Guido and Maria were first; they lived in the house. They ran to the table as the pasta dish came out of the kitchen. Alfredo and Mario were next in line, their parents behind them. "What kind of Ravioli is that?" exclaimed Maria. "I've never seen Ravioli like that!" "It's not Ravioli, it's manicotti," explained Mario's mom. Alfredo and Mario looked at each other and smiled. "We didn't think to ask this question," said Alfredo.

"We didn't know there was something other than Ravioli. I don't know what it is," said Mario. "But let's make the best of it," suggested Alfredo. His message was clear, even if unstated. Their goal was to get in line first for the Ravioli. Since they had no control over making the Ravioli, they'd enjoy what was being served. They'd be positive.

They believed they had been successful because they learned from their previous experience, worked as a team and had a good quality discussion. The experience made them stronger, more positive and able to deal with difficult challenges in securing Ravioli. Rather than blaming each other for not thinking to ask a question about the type of pasta served, they learned from this experience and added it to their menu of questions for future use.

Then Guido and Maria started screaming. They wanted Ravioli, not manicotti! Their mom took them outside, where they continued complaining loudly, bitterly. "We wanted Ravioli! We live here!" While they cried outside, people were inside, helping themselves to manicotti. Alfredo and Mario worked around the table, also helping themselves to the meal, along with the adults and the other children. Some people were gentle in the approach. Others were rude. Even some adults acted like children, filling up their plate and talking and running with food in their mouths.

Alfredo and Mario decided they'd never want to act like the adults who behave like children; nor did they want to behave like Maria and Guido, even though they understand their disappointment. Alfredo and Mario knew the unexpected could happen in getting the Ravioli. Alfredo and Mario modeled themselves after the mature adults calmly walking around the table. When Guido and Maria returned, the manicotti was gone. They had overcome their disappointment and decided to eat. But now it was too late. They began crying again.

"All the manicottis are gone," they shrieked. They missed their opportunity because they were outside crying about Ravioli. Alfredo and Mario each had a manicotti left on their plate. So they both stood up and walked over to Guido and Maria and offered them their food. Guido and Maria took the plates and ran into the kitchen to eat the manicotti.

Alfredo and Mario experienced a sense of déjà vu and smiled. They realized that Maria and Guido had not yet recovered from the experience to learn lessons and react positively. Later, as Alfredo and Mario were leaving, Maria and Guido came over and thanked them for sharing their manicotti. Guido said, "I thought the both of you took the last manicotti, but you offered your manicotti to us. We won't forget that you helped us when we needed to be helped. Thank you for thinking of us."

"One day we will see you again at dinner eating Ravioli instead of manicotti," Alfredo said. Maria and Guido agreed and smiled. On the way home, Alfredo and Mario reflected about what happened. After the experience with Uncle Vito, reflection became a part of their routine after any event. "You know, I think that maybe we should have been clear with sharing our manicotti with Maria and Guido," said Alfredo. "I think since they ran away, they misunderstood our intentions."

"Were we smiling, or did we have a serious look on our faces?" asked Mario. "I'm not sure. I thought I was smiling." "Well, I thought I had a serious look on my face." "Well, if we had one of each, maybe they were unclear about our intentions. If we were to do this again we should spell out why we're giving it to them."

"We did not spend time saying something like, 'I'm sorry that there are no manicotti for you,'" said Mario. "'Let us share our manicotti with you. We already ate enough.'" The boys decided from this day forward they would communicate their intentions clearly, succinctly and look a person straight in the eye. "That's good," Mario said. "I think they were able to thank us because we shared the manicotti with them and we established a relationship." Alfredo agreed. "Because we assisted in making it a better event for them, they were able to stop dwelling on what happened, take time to remove any anger, think clearer and have a better result."

After this new experience, they realized it is better to win people over by being friendly instead of being selfish, obnoxious and demanding. They also decided not to be self-absorbed in their own importance. "You know, Mario, I have another thought about the look on our faces. I wasn't sure if we were smiling or not. I think we should always smile and maintain direct eye contact with people. It's a nice way to be friendly to someone. It eases any initial tension in first meeting people. This way, we don't have to re-member if we smiled, since we always smile."

"That's good thinking Alfredo. You know I have seen some people smile. But they are not real smiles. We need to make sure our smiles are genuine, real and sincere." "Good, let's do it!" At home the next day, after Alfred and Mario had dinner, Uncle Vito came over and brought gelato. They ran to him and gave him happy hugs. They all sat down and ate the gelato and laughed.

They thanked Uncle Vito for coming over. They smiled, looked him straight in the eye when they spoke. "We wanted you to know that we were upset with you when you ate the Ravioli that Sunday," said Alfredo. "But we have learned from it and view it as positive learning experience." Added Mario, "So, Uncle Vito, thank you for making us better because it forced us to become stronger and more positive."

Alfredo and Mario had learned at an early age how to turn a negative into a positive. Uncle Vito smiled and gladly took credit. "I knew you guys had it in you." This conversation led Alfredo and Mario to start developing the first set of Ravioli Rules. The basic principles involved what they learned in the two weeks from the lost Ravioli to the manicotti dinner.

- You will lose your opportunity to get the Ravioli if you are asleep. If you snooze, you lose.

- Don't blame other people if they get the Ravioli and you don't.

- If you think you should automatically get the Ravioli without working for it, your expectations are too high.

- If you lost the Ravioli, you never owned it anyway.

- If you don't get the Ravioli the first time, it is not the end of the world.

- If you didn't get the Ravioli, take time to reflect on why you missed the opportunity, and put plans in action to get the Ravioli the next time.

- Always have a backup plan.

- React positively if the Ravioli has been substituted, even if you hungered for the Ravioli.

- Anyone can get the Ravioli; you just have to work around the table with others.

- Learn from those that act immature – which may have been the way you previously acted. Reflect on your process on how to get the Ravioli. Reflection will assist you in learning how to secure the Ravioli.

- People may misunderstand your best intentions to share the Ravioli. You may experience a lack of appreciation in sharing. It is only through a good level of communication that you will understand each other.

- Watch others and learn from ladies and gentlemen in getting the Ravioli. If you watch the best and, in turn, think like the best, it will help you improve. You could even be better than the best.

- Smile when you see the Ravioli.

They congratulated themselves and then wondered: If this is what we could learn in two Sundays, think of what we could learn every Sunday in our life when it is Ravioli day – a lifetime of lessons.

RAVIOLI - THE LEARNING

When Alfredo and Mario learned how to get the Ravioli, they reached their next stage of development. They enjoyed eating the Ravioli and being a part of the celebration. They now embarked on a new journey, a new challenge. They wanted to make the Ravioli, and to be the best at it.

Ravioli Rule: Establish a goal, a vision and a desire to reach the Ravioli.

The boys were eager and excited to learn how to make the Ravioli. "We have plenty of relatives who know how to make the Ravioli," they thought. "It can't be hard. And we know that if we don't get it right the first time, we will just try it again until we get it right."

Ravioli Rule: Learn from the Ravioli-making experience of others who thoroughly know the process.

Alfredo said, "Let's go see **Aunt Concetta.** She always makes good Ravioli, and she laughs all of the time. She likes us. Let's talk to her." Mario agreed. "Good idea. She likes it when we're at her house, eating her Ravioli."

Aunt Concetta was happy to see them. She offered some milk and biscotti. "This is a fine day," she said. "To what do I owe the honor of this visit?" Alfredo answered with a smile. "We love your Ravioli. You make the best. We want you to teach us how to make Ravioli. We want to learn from the best."

The boys were taken aback by Aunt Concetta's indignant response. "You come here out of the blue and expect me to stop what I am doing? To teach you how to make Ravioli?! Do you know how long it took me to make Ravioli? You can't learn it in a day! Even my two daughters don't know how. I tried teaching them, but they lost their patience. If they couldn't do it, how can you? Besides, you are too young. It requires the wisdom that comes from experience and maturity. Also, everyone knows that men can't make Ravioli. It's not in their blood. Have you seen any man make Ravioli? Have you seen your father? Are you playing a joke on me?"

Appropriate to their back-up plan, Mario and Alfredo remained calm. They reasoned with their aunt. "We are mature and interested in learning." "No!" responded Aunt Concetta. "It requires years of experience. Now go! Find something else to do! Go out and play!"

The boys left and discussed the conversation they just had with Aunt Concetta. They were glad they stayed calm and didn't voice harsh words. That would have created more hostility. Mario said, "You know counting to ten was a big help to stay calm." "I know, said Alfredo, I counted to ten about 6 times.

They thought about what their Aunt said about her daughters. Maybe the girls weren't interested in learning how to make the Ravioli. Or, maybe the reason they didn't want to learn was because of their mom.

"That could be true," said Alfredo. "Imagine the lack of support that cousins Maria and Alberta received. If the girls did something wrong, Aunt Concetta would yell at them." "Yes, I can hear her now," said Mario. "'You're not doing it right! This is how you do it!'" "She has no patience with anyone," said Alfredo. "She stifles the learning process. Her approach and manners stop people from wanting to learn how to make the Ravioli. That's why the girls moved out and learned how to make Ravioli on their own. It came from their own experience." "Now their mom doesn't even talk to them," said Mario. "She is upset they know how to make the Ravioli and she had nothing to do with it. Still, when all the relatives are around Aunt Concetta, she takes credit for teaching them how to make the Ravioli."

Alfredo and Mario placed observations on their list of learning behaviors. They did not want to treat anyone like the way Aunt Concetta treated them. They learned that some people with Ravioli-making experience might want to intimidate you. "Let's not act that way," they agreed.

Ravioli Rule: Don't be intimidated by people who yell at you and tell you that you can't make the Ravioli. In the future, if someone asks you for advice on how to make the Ravioli, encourage him or her to learn.

They decided to visit Aunt Sophia, who lived right down the street. She was happy to see the boys. She's much calmer than Aunt Concetta. Later, they felt they should have visited Aunt Sophia first. When they asked her about how to make Ravioli, she was flattered. Then she calmly described the process.

"You boys may not be aware of the time it takes to make the Ravioli," she said. "You have to make the dough, then let it rest, and then you have to roll it out, shape it and form it. You have to make the filling a day in advance. Then you have to stuff the pasta and seal them and let them rest. Then you have to make the sauce. This is a very long task, boys. I hope my directions help you."

She talked for a very long time about the minute details. "It takes days to make the right Ravioli. I appreciate your interest, but I just don't have the time today. I have to go shopping. My day is filled. Because making Ravioli is so long of a task, you have to make an appointment with me all day long, and because the weather is nice I will be outside. Maybe when the winter comes you can meet with me. We'll spend the day together to make the Ravioli. I'll see you now. Bye, bye boys." She led them out.

"She didn't even listen to us," said Mario. "We could not get a word in at all. She just talked the whole time with so much detail. She must have talked for 30 minutes." "And if it takes so long, how does she have time to make the Ravioli in the winter time," wondered Alfredo. "It doesn't make sense. It can't take that long. If Aunt Concetta says it takes lots of experience why can't Aunt Sophia make it without so much drama? It seems that she wanted to make it sound like a long and dramatic process with a lot of detail."

Ravioli Rule: *Explain the Ravioli-making process with the big picture first and then when they grasp the concept give them more details. Not the other way around.*

Next, the boys went to visit Aunt Josephine. She, too, welcomed them with biscotti and milk. "It is so nice of you to visit. What can I do for you boys? Did you just want to say 'hi' to your Aunt?" "We would like to learn how to make Ravioli," the boys revealed.

"Well boys, it is perfect that you are here, because timing is everything," she said. "I need to start making Ravioli for a dinner two days from now. You can help get it started." She took them into the kitchen. "Here are the flour, the eggs, the bowls and the ricotta cheese for the filling. You boys could make it now. I have to run to the store and I will be back in five hours. By the time I return, I expect that you will have the Ravioli made."

She put on her coat and ran out the door. The boys were stunned. "How could she do this to us," complained Alfredo. "It was like we asked her how to make it and she doesn't even show us."

"Not only doesn't she show us, she gives us the materials and then she runs off," said Mario. "She dumped it on us and ran away. We are in the same position as we were before we asked her. We have all these materials at home. We could do the same thing."

"I know," said Alfredo. "We are looking for someone to coach us to success and all she did was throw stuff at us and expect it to be done. There are no rules, no directions, and zero guidance. How can we get this done? She overwhelmed us with stuff we don't even understand."

The boys thought about it for a bit and decided to give it a try. They started with the eggs and flour. How many eggs go into each pound of flour? They looked around the kitchen for Ravioli directions, opening drawers and pulling out papers, looking for a recipe. After four hours, they decided this was not for them. They needed some guidance, some rules – a plan. It seemed that no one wanted to share a plan or give up a family secret. "Maybe we should just stop. Every time we turn around, it seems that we are doomed to failure. Our family is not supportive or encouraging," said Alfredo.

Aunt Josephine returned from the store. "Hi boys, how is it going? Is the Ravioli all made?" The boys were afraid of what would happen next. "What! – I give you my best materials, my best ingredients, the finest in the land, and you have done absolutely nothing with it," Aunt Josephine exclaimed. "I leave you for five hours and nothing is done. How do you expect to make the Ravioli if you don't try? You should have figured it out by now. You expect me to lead you by the hand. I left you with everything you needed and you don't live up to your promises. I am very disappointed."

The boys concluded that Aunt Josephine is a person who knows how to make the Ravioli, but provides little direction and poor communication. The D&R (Dump and Run) mentality is common among poor communicators who are unclear about their own direction.

Ravioli Rule: If someone asks you how to make the Ravioli, provide clear directions. Give them the complete recipe, the goals and objectives so that it is clearly understood. Give the directions and advice up front to guide them, not after everything is made.

Next, they visited Uncle Aldo. They asked him for the Ravioli recipe. "Boys," he said, "you don't need to learn how to make the Ravioli, because I am always here. As long as you have me around you don't need to make the Ravioli. Don't worry, I know everything about the Ravioli." "But that's why we want to learn from you," said Alfredo. "Show us how to make the Ravioli," said Mario. "Don't worry about it. Uncle Aldo will always be here for you." "Yes, we know you are here, but let's do this together."

"Boys, put your faith and trust in me. I'll deliver for you. When do you want me to serve the Ravioli for you? You tell me when you want to have them for dinner and I'll have them there. Do you want them for dinner tonight or tomorrow night?" "We want to be there as you make the Ravioli, before you serve them for dinner," said Mario.

Uncle Aldo said, "Boys, don't worry, you never have to learn how to make the Ravioli because Uncle Aldo will make them for you. Why do you have to do all that work when I am right here at your call to make them for you? If you need to eat the Ravioli for lunch or dinner, just let me know and I will make sure I am there for you."

The boys thanked him for his graciousness, wished him a good day and left. On their way home, they concluded that some people who know how to make the Ravioli might never share the recipe. The reason is because they like being in charge and do not want to share their knowledge. They like having others dependent on them.

Ravioli Rule: Share the Ravioli-making process when you are asked, and you may gain a new relationship in Ravioli-making.

The boys now visited Aunt Louisa and asked her the question. "You want me to share with you the family secret of how we make Ravioli?" she said. "Oh, no you don't. The other family members have wanted to learn how to make my Ravioli and I have never given them the recipe. So now someone is sending you over to me to get this recipe. No way! I didn't give it to them and they are not going to send over two little boys to get the family recipe. It has been preserved for five generations and handed from daughter to daughter. I'm sorry, boys, but I will take my recipe to my grave."

This time the boys concluded that some people who know how to make the Ravioli like to keep it a big secret. Unfortunately, they aren't preserving their knowledge and experience for anyone.

Ravioli Rule: After you have learned how to make the Ravioli and have years of experience, share your Ravioli making knowledge with others so they can learn from your positive experiences.

They next went to Uncle Peppino. He was happy to see them. When they asked him about the Ravioli, he said, "You know, boys, to make the Ravioli you need to know the history. All people have different versions of the history, but I know where it started, because my family handed it down to me. They told me the origins."

"It began long ago in a small town in Italy…," he said. Then he talked on and on. He spoke at length about the potential for making and eating the greatest Ravioli, but he was speaking in generalities, providing no detail or reason. The boys lost interest and decided to leave. He was still talking as they passed through the door. By now, he was repeating himself. "It began long ago in a small town in Italy… ." Alfredo said, "I guess we should expect some people who make the Ravioli to talk endlessly about the history of Ravioli. But they lose focus on why you came to see them."

Ravioli Rule: Remember the importance of the Ravioli history, but don't get lost in the history, otherwise there will not be a Ravioli future.

The boys continued their quest. "We are not giving up, we must persevere," said Alfredo. "Every time we visit someone, they have a reason why they can't share it or why we don't have the skills to do it on our own." "This is disappointing, but let's keep going," said Mario.

Ravioli rule: When it looks like you will never make the Ravioli, keep going. Don't resign but be resilient and recover. The result is worth it.

"Let's go visit Aunt Carmina," Alfredo suggested.

When the boys told her they wanted to make Ravioli, she said, "Oh boys, it is so simple." The boys looked at each other. Finally, they were going to get the straight scoop. "Just take a handful of flour and place it on the counter," Aunt Carmina explained. "Then, take a cup of water, one egg and mix it together. It's real easy. Let it rest for half an hour. While it's resting, make the ricotta stuffing. Take one cup of ricotta cheese, one egg, some mozzarella cheese, some Romano cheese, some parsley, add it all together and mix it up. By the time you've done that, you can pull out the dough, roll it out and then stuff the squares or circles with the ricotta cheese and seal it with a fork and egg wash. That's it. Then you put them in the boiling water and wait for the Ravioli to get done. Pull them out of the water and serve with a sauce. That's all there is to it. Now you have it, so off with you and make the Ravioli."

The boys went home. Their mom was not there, so they hurried to the kitchen and started making the Ravioli. They took a handful of flour and placed it on the counter, as Aunt Carmina had instructed. They got one of their dad's coffee cups and filled it with water and got the one jumbo egg left in the refrigerator. They took the handful of flour—small in their little hands—and spread it out so they could mix the water in the center of the well. They added the water and the egg and beat it in the center well. Then they started to pull the flour together. They were getting excited. They were making the Ravioli!

But as they continued to pull in the flour, the texture was still very mushy. It did not look like Ravioli dough at all. They kept working it, becoming increasingly frustrated. The dough was sticky and did not roll out softly. They put the Ravioli dough in a bag and went back to Aunt Carmina, to show what they had done and to ask for advice. "Boys," she said, "you did this all wrong. This dough has too much water in it. You need more flour. I told you to use a handful of flour. See, like this."

She went to her own flour mixture and inserted her hands. She must have picked up at least three cups with her large hands – far more than what the boys could have picked with their smaller hands. She then got a glass measuring cup, filled it with water and added to the flour mixture. She took one egg, mixed it in the well and then, in five minutes, she mixed up the pasta dough. "See," she said. "What is so hard about that?"

The boys then realized that a visual picture explained a lot more than general directions, which lacked clarity. They thanked her and left. Alfredo said to Mario, "I wish she had been this precise before." Mario said, "Yes, our making of the Ravioli was bad because of the inaccurate and inadequate information provided by Aunt Carmina. We also needed to learn to ask questions to confirm and clarify what Aunt Carmina meant."

Ravioli Rule: Learn to ask the right questions during the Ravioli-making process. Ensure the directions and information are accurate and not subject to interpretation. Have a quality discussion.

They next visited Uncle Bruno and asked him for his Ravioli recipe. "I never made the Ravioli," he said. "I have the plans and the recipes and several variations, but I never had the time to make it. The plans are sitting up there in that cupboard. Let me get them. See, they are still on an old piece of paper."He perused the plans, and then placed them back in the cupboard. "Oh, it's too much work. I can pull out frozen Ravioli and make them quicker," he said.

So the boys left and determined that, with everyone making the Ravioli, Uncle Bruno had lost interest in the making.

Ravioli Rule: Making Ravioli plans are not enough. You must act and learn how to make the Ravioli, otherwise you will never enjoy the real Ravioli.

The boys next visited Aunt Lia and asked her how to make Ravioli. Aunt Lia, who was 90 years old, said, "Your timing is just off. I make Ravioli twice a year and freeze them and use them all year long. I just made my semi-annual Ravioli. Let me show you."

She showed them the hundreds of Ravioli she made all around the house. Every table, bed and flat surface was taken up with Ravioli of every size and shape. Amazed, the boys asked, "How did you make all of this?" "With lots of planning and energy," replied Aunt Lia. "Once you are used to the process, it is easy."

Ravioli Rule: Great Ravioli makers have a relentless level of strength, determination, endurance, resilience, intensity and energy. Like rapidly boiling water that never stops. They also use the Ravioli process and years of Ravioli experience to accomplish the results.

The boys went home and were talking in the kitchen about how to make the Ravioli. From the dining room, their Mom heard them and decided to take some action, since they were interested in making the Ravioli.

She asked the boys if they wanted to play or if they wanted to learn something. "It's your choice," she said. The boys eagerly said they wanted to learn. "Then I have good news for you. Today, I thought about making Ravioli." The boys exchanged excited glances. "If you are interested in learning how to make the Ravioli, I can show you."

"We would love to learn", the boys said. So, Mom started to show them how to make the Ravioli. "Boys, I have been making it for years and my mom showed me. It is really easy to make. The good news is that you have the desire." Their Mom took out a five-pound bag of flour, a big cup to be filled with water and a dozen eggs. The boys were wide-eyed with anticipation yet scared because of the volume of materials. She looked at them. "It is not a mountain of flour and eggs. Just take it in steps. I will show you."

Ravioli Rule: *Making the Ravioli is not making the impossible. Learn it in bits, and once you are comfortable you will master the art of making the Ravioli.*

She put on her apron and got out her wooden roller and flat wooden board so she could roll out her Ravioli, and she also got some spoons, forks, the Ravioli press, some semolina flour, wax paper, towels to be moistened, ricotta cheese, parsley and mozzarella cheese.

Ravioli Rule: *Making Ravioli the right way requires the right equipment and the right ingredients.*

Next, Mom took out her Ravioli recipe. "This is the guiding plan to make the Ravioli. If you want to make the right Ravioli you also need to have a plan, a blueprint, the outline of the direction. This is the plan. I've have had it for years." She placed the plan on the table.

"This is called a recipe," she said. "It is the process from start to finish on how to make the Ravioli. See, it includes how to make the dough and how to make the stuffing. Directions are clear and concise. It even has pictures on how to make the Ravioli step by step. Just follow this recipe, as I have done for many years, and you will make the Ravioli."

Ravioli Rule: *The right Ravioli recipe is a very clear and precise process so you can make the Ravioli the right way.*

The boys thanked Mom for sharing the plan with them. Mario said, "Thanks Mom, now that you shared the Ravioli-making process and your Ravioli vision, I now understand the 'how'." "Yeah," Alfredo said, "we are ready to make the Ravioli."

Ravioli Rule: *Share the recipe plan with the people who will make the Ravioli. They will fully understand how to make Ravioli and will be grateful.*

Mom knew her boys were interested in making the Ravioli. She must have had at least three calls from her sisters and other family members that the boys were looking to make the Ravioli. She didn't let on that she knew about all these visits. "Boys, you do know that if you ever want to know how to make the Ravioli, all you need to do is ask me. I will show you. If you like, I could show you other recipes as well – but it is your choice."

Ravioli Rule: Sometimes we need to understand that, as Ravioli teachers, we shouldn't yell at potential Ravioli makers but coach them to Ravioli success. Sometimes, for potential Ravioli makers, the answer to learning how to make the Ravioli is right in front of them. All they need to do is ask.

As her sons' learning progressed, Mom said, "You have watched me make the Ravioli. You have the recipe and the visual experience of watching me. I even let you roll out the dough and I helped you with the ricotta stuffing. Maybe one day you could make the Ravioli by yourself. What do you think?"

The boys told her that they'd love to be their own Ravioli makers. Mom said, "Great, maybe next week you can make the Ravioli."

Ravioli Rule: After someone watches you make the Ravioli, encourage them to learn how to make the Ravioli by letting them practice making the Ravioli on their own.

The following week, the boys decided to make the Ravioli. Their Mom thought it would be best if she let them learn on their own. If they were younger, she would stick by and supervise, but she had confidence in them. She was going to stand in another room while they learned on their own. It would be best because if they make mistakes and fix them – that's the most effective learning method.

Ravioli Rule: Ravioli makers need to learn on their own and from their experiences.

When Mom put out all the ingredients, the boys feared that it may be too much for them. They became apprehensive. Mom saw their anxiety. "Boys, remember, make this in bits, small pieces at a time. I know it looks overwhelming but, remember, all people feel this way when they start something new. It is normal; you are not alone. If you are scared, it will get in the way of making the Ravioli and you will lose your focus. Learn to overcome the anxiety. Smile and work through it and you will be successful in making the Ravioli."

Ravioli Rule: Overcome the anxiety of making the Ravioli. You will kick yourself if someone else takes the chance and makes the Ravioli. When you succeed, you will say, "I can't believe I was afraid of making the Ravioli. It was so easy."

The boys started to make the Ravioli. First, they placed their plans on the table and organized the ingredients. The recipe had directions for making different types of Ravioli, the making of meatballs and sausage, and the process for making a variety of sauces to serve with the Ravioli. They came upon a startling discovery. They could not make all of these things in one day. They realized that not everything is a priority. The purpose of today is to learn how to make the Ravioli and become confident in this process. Cramming all of this into one session was too much. So they decided the only priority for today was learning how to make the Ravioli. Creating all of these different Ravioli and sauces at the same time is a long process that they would learn at a later time.

Ravioli Rule: Everything is not important. Decide what is important for today. If you do too much at one time, you will become overwhelmed, frustrated and lose interest, resulting in incomplete or poorly made Ravioli.

So, the boys looked at the Ravioli recipe and realized there were several steps. There were two main processes: the creation of the Ravioli dough and the creation of the stuffing. All of the ingredients for both were out on the table. According to the recipe, after the dough was kneaded and rolled it had to rest for 30 minutes, to allow the gluten to become elastic, which would improve the rolling of the dough. The boys made their plan efficient by making the Ravioli dough first and then making the ricotta stuffing while the dough rested.

Ravioli Rule: Some parts of the entire Ravioli-making process may need to be completed first before moving onto the next step.

After about an hour, they made their first Ravioli. After a lot of hard work, teamwork and patience, the first Ravioli was pressed together. "Let's not cook all of them," suggested Alfredo. "Let's take just one or two to cook and see what happens." "I'm scared," Mario said.

"We should not be afraid to see if it works," said Alfredo. "It is better to try it on one, rather than on all of them. This way we could tweak and fix it on the other Ravioli. It is a good test."

Ravioli Rule: Don't be afraid to test anything, and test a small sample when you make the Ravioli for the first time, to see if they meet expectations.

The boys placed a couple of Ravioli in a small pot of water. After a few minutes, the edges started to come apart. When they were making the Ravioli, they didn't use egg wash to seal the edges. As a result, the edges became loose in the boiling water. They realized that quality is important, even when rushing through the excitement of making the Ravioli.

Ravioli Rule: Don't risk the quality of the Ravioli to expedite the making.

So, the boys fixed the edges on the rest of the Ravioli and now they put 20 Ravioli in a pot of boiling water. Then they taste-tested the Ravioli. The result was sticky and mushy, because the amount of Ravioli was too much for the amount of water. They used one quart for two pounds of Ravioli, when five to six quarts is necessary for every pound of pasta.

Ravioli Rule: The Ravioli will be useless if it is pushed beyond the limits of the appropriate water to Ravioli ratio. Don't put too many Ravioli in the water. Make sure there is enough water for the amount of Ravioli.

The boys filled up a big pot of water. When the water was on a gentle rolling boil, they dropped in the Ravioli, one at a time. When the Ravioli floated to the top, they waited one minute and pulled the Ravioli out of the pot and put them in a bowl. They tasted one. It tasted good. "But let's ask an expert," said Mario.

Just then, Mom walked into the kitchen. "How is it going, boys?" "You're just in time," said Alfredo. "Try our Ravioli and let us know what you think."

Ravioli Rule: *Test the Ravioli on a sincere friend who will give you an honest appraisal, as well as constructive criticism.*

"These are excellent," Mom said. "You boys did a wonderful job your first time making the Ravioli. You followed the rules and created the Ravioli. You should be very proud!" The boys were beaming. After all the frustration and criticism in their search for guidance, they were now assuming the role of Ravioli makers. If only their Aunt's and Uncle's could see them now.

"Let's celebrate your success!" their Mom exclaimed. "I will set a table and make a butter, cheese and garlic sauce."

Ravioli Rule: *Celebrate the success of even the first step. It will encourage you to continue to succeed. Success breeds success.*

As they ate, they discussed the Ravioli making-process. "What do you think you did right and wrong," Mom asked. "Maybe we could have timed things a little better or prepared the mix in advance, so that we could save time in the process," said Alfredo. "Indeed," said their proud mother. "Always remember to spend time reflecting on the Ravioli result, to see if there is room for improvement."

Ravioli Rule: *Make time to follow up, review and reflect on the results of Ravioli making, so you can look to improve this process and make even better Ravioli.*

So, the next Saturday the boys were out walking around. They wanted to get something to eat, and they were talking about the success they had in their first real attempt at making Ravioli. They reviewed the events and went over each step in detail.

A man named Joe overheard their conversation. "Excuse me, men, I couldn't help but hear how excited you are about making Ravioli for the first time," he said. "You know, I make the best Ravioli in town. My relatives say mine is the best, and served with the best sauce. It took me a long time to figure out how to make the right Ravioli. They now call me a Ravioli maestro."

"Wow!" said the boys, "What did you do to make the best Ravioli?" "It's easy. If you are interested, I will show you. Come with me. I don't live far from here." At his house, Joe said, "Sit here in the living room, and I will soon make the Ravioli." "But we want to watch how you make it," said Alfredo. Joe laughed. "If you're that interested, then come into the kitchen." Joe put on his apron, put on the hot water and brought out a pot for the sauce. "How long have you been making Ravioli," Mario asked. "Oh, about 15 years, and now I am the best Ravioli maker," Joe said.

The boys intently watched Joe's process. They were surprised that while the water boiled, Joe had yet to make his dough. Then they watched as he went to the freezer, pulled out a package of frozen Ravioli and placed them in the hot water. The boys looked at each. "Wow," said Alfredo. "He is so good that he freezes his Ravioli." "Yes, like one of our relatives," said Mario.

As the water boiled, Joe took out a jar of sauce from the refrigerator and placed it in his pot. "He is very organized," observed Alfredo. "It appears that he has been prepared for moments like this, so that he can enjoy the Ravioli one day at a time," said Mario, as he watched Joe work.

The Ravioli and the sauce were ready. Joe placed everything in the dining room. The boys began to eat. However, the Ravioli tasted different. So did the sauce. Nothing seemed homemade. The boys questioned him about his method. "How do you make your Ravioli," asked Alfredo. "What type of flour do you use, and do you use jumbo or extra large eggs?" Joe laughed. "I buy the Ravioli and the sauce. I don't have time to make it. I found the best place to buy them, and then I make them myself by putting them in the water. The jar of bought sauce makes it easy. My family loves my Ravioli. They say it is the best."

This wasn't quite what the boys were looking for. They finished their meal, thanked the gentleman for a fine Ravioli meal and left.

Ravioli Rule: People who brag about making the best Ravioli may have a different perception than you. In these instances, don't make fun of them, just smile and make them feel good, otherwise they would be embarrassed.

The boys went to a nearby café for espresso and cannoli. The talked about Ravioli and about all of their recent experiences. Someone seated nearby overhead them talking about the Ravioli-making process. He talked to the boys about his own Ravioli. He spoke of the basics—rolling out the dough, and the eggs and cheese—and expressed opinions about the overall process and the best ingredients. He went into detail about air-drying the dough, and usage of fresh eggs from a farm and fresh water from a spring. He exhibited great confidence. Surely, he had to be an expert, the boys thought.

"I could help you make the Ravioli," he told them. "How long have you been making Ravioli," Alfredo asked. "I never made Ravioli," the man revealed. "I just watch people make Ravioli. That's how I became an expert."

Ravioli Rule: Some people like to exaggerate their knowledge; don't let them dupe you. They offer lots of advice, suggestions, options, and schemes. If they have no experience or knowledge, they can't provide sound advice.

The next Saturday the boys went to work making the Ravioli. They decided that they would make it every Saturday. They believed that continued practice would give them more experience and make them master Ravioli makers.

Ravioli Rule: To become a great Ravioli maker you need to practice, practice, practice.

The boys put their plans together in the morning. They wrote up so many plans that it would take them all of Saturday. While they thought this was a worthwhile endeavor, they found they could have written the plans in fewer words. They were dotting every "i" and crossing every "t" and it stopped them from the practical experience of making the Ravioli.

Ravioli Rule: Planning is important, but don't over-plan. Don't get lost in minutia.

The boys rolled out the dough and flattened it out, and were ready to prepare and stuff the Ravioli. Alfredo placed the ricotta stuffing mixture in the dough, and Mario sealed the edges. They placed the Ravioli in the boiling water. Once cooked, the Ravioli was placed in a dish, with butter and cheese sauce. After the first bite, they spit out the Ravioli.

"This tastes terrible!" shouted Mario. The ricotta cheese had gone sour in the refrigerator from last week. "We should have tasted the cheese before we put it in the Ravioli," said Alfredo. "We failed. I can't believe we got this far and made this kind of simple mistake." "It's ok," said Mario. "Failing is a powerful learning tool. Let's not let it get us down. We can learn from this.

We need to put in a quality check to make sure the ricotta is fresh and maintains the quality."

Ravioli Rule: When you find an error affecting the Ravioli, don't get mad. Rather, institute a new rule to fix the problem. For instance, test the ricotta stuffing for quality and freshness before placing it in the dough.

The lunch was ruined. The boys came up with an alternate plan. "Let's make the dried penne pasta with the same butter and cheese sauce," suggested Mario.

"Yeah", said Alfredo, "and for a special flavor we will add peas and prosciutto."

It took them about 15 minutes to prepare their lunch. As they ate, they were proud that they found a substitute.

Ravioli Rule: Don't let a setback stop you from achieving your goal. Stopping won't lead to success. If the Ravioli doesn't work, make alternative pasta.

The next Saturday, they made a large pot of tomato sauce, which they divided into several portions. The idea was to freeze it for future meals.

They made a meatless sauce – a marinara sauce. They started with the fresh tomatoes from the garden. They pureed them and separated the skins from the seeds. Next, they browned some extra virgin olive oil in a pot with some fresh garlic. At the precise moment, they added the sauce. It sizzled when it joined the fresh olive oil. Then they added tomato paste, to thicken the sauce. They also carefully added salt, pepper, garlic powder, oregano and Italian seasoning –adding too much of each would overpower the sauce. You can add more ingredients such as sun-dried tomatoes, fresh basil leaves, but don't put in too much.

Ravioli Rule: The right chemistry of ingredients makes a good sauce and improves the Ravioli. The ingredients can change, but there should always be the right chemistry. The sauce should not be overpowering but complement the Ravioli. The sauce is like a team, all ingredients work together to enhance the quality of the sauce and the Ravioli.

The following week the boys tried the same sauce and followed everything exactly the same way. But this time, they tried something a bit different: They thought if they let the sauce cook a little longer, it would enhance the flavor of all the ingredients. However, they didn't keep a close watch on the sauce. It was overdone. It burned because of the thickening at the bottom of the pot. The sauce needed to be closely watched and regularly stirred.

Ravioli Rule: *Stay involved in the making of the sauce. Know when the sauce and the Ravioli are done. Keep your eye on both.*

The next weekend, they opted to make a simple sauce. A good sauce would enhance the Ravioli they were striving to make. They felt this was a good approach, and they'd celebrate their achievement with a nice lunch, a bottle of wine and some bread – and then finish the experience with a nice after-lunch nap.

When they started making their Ravioli, a neighbor walked in. She watched them make the Ravioli and advised that the water needed salt. "Why?" the boys asked. The neighbor said she didn't know; she only knew that it was necessary. And she went on and on about this. In the meantime, the sauce started burning and the water almost completely evaporated. Too much time was spent on the salt discussion.

Ravioli Rule: *Make sure you focus your efforts on the important things. Getting lost in minutia and debate while the sauce and Ravioli are cooking is immaterial to making Ravioli.*

The boys were gaining confidence. Each week, their Ravioli was getting better and better. Now, they wanted to make Ravioli using whole-wheat flour. They put out the ingredients and kneaded the dough. The new ingredient involved the same amount as previous flour ingredients. However, the kneading of the whole-wheat flour dough seemed to take forever. The boys discovered that because the whole-wheat flour is a heavier flour, it takes longer to knead the dough to make it as elastic as regular flour. The texture and content are not the same, and it significantly impacts the result. So they promised themselves that, in the future, they'd better understand the affect of any ingredient changes.

Ravioli Rule: *A good Ravioli maker understands the strengths and weaknesses of all ingredients and knows the affect a slight change in one of the ingredients has on the Ravioli-making process. They will always remember this as the whole-wheat flour lesson.*

For their next step, the boys made a traditional meat sauce – with meatballs, sausage, the works. They gathered their ingredients on Saturday morning. They made the meatballs (one pound of meat, garlic powder, milk, breadcrumbs, cheeses, one egg for every pound of meat and some onion flakes). They made 40 meatballs and started to fry them, along with the sausage. When the meat was cooked, they added it to the tomato sauce mixture to simmer. Next, they made the Ravioli, which they added to the boiling water. Once done and drained, the Ravioli were ready to serve.

They tasted the sauce; it needed to be cooked some more. Meanwhile, they had to keep their Ravioli warm. By this time, they were hungry and ready to eat. But they had to wait. This experience was another lesson learned: Timing the readiness of the sauce with the cooked Ravioli is critical.

Ravioli Rule: Timing is the key in making the Ravioli and the meat sauce. Know how much time it takes to have all the components of the Ravioli dinner ready at the same time.

The boys now were becoming more confident in their Ravioli-making abilities. It was time to try out their skills on a family dinner. First, they'd invite immediate family members on a Sunday. A few weeks later, they'd invite all of their aunts and uncles. They felt that this plan was in line with the Ravioli rules. They'd test the process first and then, after success, they'd roll it out to the entire family. But with the first family dinner, they knew they needed to establish an overall goal.

Ravioli Rule: The goal is making the perfect Ravioli and serving the Ravioli with a great sauce in a simple and elegant presentation.

The day before the family dinner, the boys made an ingredient list: tomato sauce, sausage, ground beef, garlic, tomato paste, ricotta cheese, flour, eggs, parsley and breadcrumbs. They checked the kitchen inventory and purchased the missing ingredients.

Their mom told them to get a little extra for backup. She told them about when their grandma found her flour container infested with bugs. Smart woman that she was, she had an uninfected backup flour container in another closet. She made it a practice to store backups in different locations. She learned this years ago from a friend, Rosemary Ravli. (Did this friend create Ravli O Li, the boys joked.) Ravli said that, her ancestors who were boat captains taught her that, instead of placing all merchandise on one boat, it is better to spread the materials over several boats. So in case one ship was damaged on the river or the ocean, they had a supply of backups.

Ravioli Rule: Don't keep all your Ravioli ingredients in one cabinet. Always have enough ingredients and multiple backups. Keep a list of your ingredients and increase the stock when the volumes are getting low.

The boys started to make the Ravioli according to the plans. They were acting on their dream: to make a real Ravioli dinner.

Ravioli Rule: When you act on something, you must have the will to achieve your goal. It becomes more than a plan; it becomes the product - the Ravioli.

Their dad came in and asked them how many Ravioli they were making. "Twenty-four," the boys estimated. "Twenty-four perfect Ravioli," dad said, as he left the kitchen. Mario looked at Alfredo. "If we're expected to make 24 perfect Ravioli, we better make extra, in case all are not perfect."

Alfredo agreed. After all, dad seemed to place strong emphasis on "perfect." Meanwhile, they had come to realize the importance of feedback: Listening is an important management tool. You're well served when you act on the advice.

Their important next step was to manage the Ravioli-making process. It began with cooking the meat and frying the sausage on Saturday. They also prepared the Ravioli filling.

This way, they could more efficiently and effectively manage the entire process on Sunday. They made filling with romano and mozzarella cheeses, eggs and parsley, then covered it and placed it in the refrigerator. The boys drained the meat on paper towels, to remove the grease, and also placed this essential ingredient in the refrigerator. On Sunday, they would make the sauce and fresh pasta.

Excited, the boys woke early Sunday morning, pulled out the meat and placed it in a pot of tomato sauce that they prepared. They added some salt, pepper and garlic powder and let the mixture simmer for about an hour. Ever diligent, they constantly stirred the sauce, so that nothing would stick to the bottom of the pot.

Oh, they were so well organized. They knew their priorities and, as such, weren't in a chaotic rush, wondering their next step. They made their Ravioli dough, inserted the ricotta cheese, and folded over the dough, cut it, and then made ridges with a special tool. Both boys made the Ravioli. Production proved smooth – Alfredo and Mario were strongly focused and operating on automatic pilot.

Next, they put the Ravioli in a pot of boiling water, watching for when they rose to the top and cooking for five minutes. They tasted one to confirm texture. They looked at each other. The perfect Ravioli!

Ravioli Rule: Manage the immediate critical issues and responsibilities. If you remain focused and pay attention to details, the Ravioli will cook perfectly.

They drained their perfect Ravioli from the water, placed it in bowl— topped with the tomato sauce—and brought their efforts to the dinner table.

There the Ravioli stood while the family was in another room, talking about life and relatives. Alfredo and Mario waited—and waited—as discussion continued. They thought the family knew the Ravioli was ready.

Finally, the family went into the dining room. But the Ravioli was no longer hot. Freshness was lost. The flavorful aroma of the hot sauce had dissipated. The boys were disappointed. They realized they should have announced the serving as soon as it was ready.

Everyone began eating. Uncle Nico came down from an upstairs nap. "Hey! How come you didn't tell me the Ravioli was ready?"

Ravioli Rule: Sometimes you need to announce your success. The Ravioli is ready, so let people know that you have completed your job and that they can start.

But there was another problem. Alfredo and Mario's dad counted the Ravioli. There were 22, not 24. Upset, he asked, "What happened to the other two? Did you eat them?"

The boys explained that they started with more. "We each ate one," said Alfredo, "and one broke apart in the water." Added Mario: "One fell down the sink when we poured the Ravioli in the colander."

Dad didn't buy excuse and preferred to accuse. "You either ate them or miscounted," he exclaimed, with a long, bony finger pointed at their young faces.

The boys were distraught. Dad's passion was terrible and troubling, but the experience gained them yet one more lesson: Any deviation from the number of Ravioli must be communicated to the Ravioli recipients. Explain the difference so that all understand the reason for variation. More importantly, the boys understood that word must be kept. Expectations must be met.

Ravioli Rule: Keep your word. When you say that you will make an exact number, stick to the promise. This fosters trust. Broken promises indicate lack of integrity.

After dinner—and after dad calmed down—Alfredo, Mario and their parents reviewed the Ravioli presentation's positives and negatives. What worked best? How could things be improved? It was a constructive session. Notes were taken, a list developed. Even preposterous ideas were entertained. All determined that testing the process on family was a good first step, a way to find weak spots and a method to fine-tune the process. The boys had a better plan of action for next time.

Ravioli Rule: Test the Ravioli on those closest. Judgment may seem harsh, but value is immeasurable.

Now that they learned to make Ravioli for a Sunday dinner for the immediate family, the boys determined their next goal: to develop a dinner for all of the family. The smaller dinner was their springboard for growth. They now set their sights on a big event. But they planned to take it in steps.

RAVIOLI – THE GROWING

So, at this point, Alfredo and Mario look toward their next challenge: a large Ravioli holiday presentation. The small Sunday dinners were training ground. They learned about the likes and dislikes, which provided them an important ingredient: practice, practice, and practice. Success taught them much, as did failure. After all, failure is a learning experience.

Ravioli Rule: *Practice leads to success and fosters even more success. This leads to increased confidence, self-esteem and pride in accomplishment. One successful Ravioli leads to another.*

The realization led to a Sunday dinner for Aunt Mia's family. As the boys attempted again to make Ravioli, they confronted another significant problem: water normally pumped in by hand had stopped. This meant water could not boil in time. More importantly, water wasn't available to make the Ravioli dough. Ravioli wasn't even made by the time guests began arriving. Mom and dad helped out the best they could. They placed appetizers in the family room while their boys scurried to the store to buy bottled water. Just as the guests were finishing the appetizers, Alfredo and Mario had rolled out and stuffed their last Ravioli and then dropped them in boiling water. Soon, dinner was ready, thanks to their resourcefulness. The guests knew nothing about the water problem. The boys were happy but exhausted, but they couldn't savor the Ravioli they had made. The experience led them to develop another rule.

Ravioli Rule: *When you improvise solutions to make the Ravioli, balance pride with practicality. If you live on the Ravioli edge, positioned close to success or failure, you need to better manage the Ravioli process.*

Every Sunday had become a big day for Alfredo and Mario—the family, too!—as the boys got better at making Ravioli. They had developed a good plan. On Saturday, they accomplished the essentials: rolling the meatballs, frying the sausage, mixing the ricotta stuffing. Early Sunday, they made the dough, let it rest, stuffed the pasta and added meat to the sauce, which they let simmer (aroma wafting though the kitchen). Further, they sliced bread and prepared a salad. They had learned how to simplify a complex process.

On one occasion, other family children—ranging in ages from two to eight—participated. But when it came time to eat the Ravioli, the children complained. "Why are they so big?!" "Can't they be smaller, so that they are easier for us to eat," one whined.

Essentially, the children didn't want their own parents to cut up the Ravioli so many times. They wanted bite-sized portions. This experience taught Alfredo and Mario another important lesson: Often, Ravioli must be customized to suit a consumer's wants and needs. Everyone wants to enjoy the Ravioli experience.

Ravioli Rule: Listen and learn from your "dinner guests." Create Ravioli designed just for them and you'll build long-term relationships.

At another Sunday dinner, the boys engaged the family in an argument – about where they should sit during the Ravioli presentation. After all, they made the Ravioli, from start to finish. Shouldn't they sit at the head of the table, in the better chairs, where they could be recognized for their hard work?

Their parents then taught them a lesson in humility. It didn't matter where they sat. The presentation of food would provide recognition enough. The boys were establishing a reputation as Ravioli makers – perfect Ravioli.

An incident underscored this lesson. One Sunday dinner, the boys—in their distribution of Ravioli—gave themselves two more Ravioli than anyone else. After all, weren't they the Ravioli makers? Weren't they entitled?

Guests noticed the discrepancy, and complained in loud voice. "Why didn't guests get the extra Ravioli," one family member demanded. Said another, "Each week, you get to make, eat and taste! These dinners are the

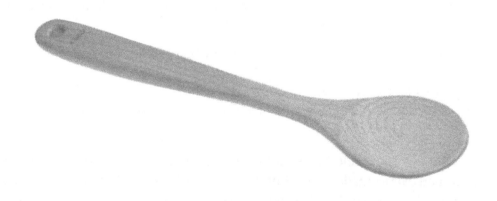

only time we get to taste the Ravioli!" "And you want special seating, too?" shouted another family member. Ah, another lesson learned for Alfredo and Mario.

Ravioli Rule: Don't worry about your seat at the table. When you give yourself priority, guests feel second rate. Guests (customers) come first, not you. Leave the ego outside of the kitchen door.

From there, dinners continued every Sunday. One on occasion, Cousin Marie, her husband and their six kids—along with Marie's two sisters and families—sat down for a dinner. All raved about the Ravioli. The women wanted to know how the boys learned to make such good Ravioli.

"It takes time," said Alfredo. "And in small steps," added Mario. "That's how we make such large dinners." Alfredo admitted that they made mistakes along the way. "But we recovered," Mario proudly proclaimed. Mistakes—both boys realized—weren't a negative. Rather, failure amounted to a learning experience. Elbow on table and palm in cheek, Mario contemplated how mistakes were a major learning tool. As if reading Mario's mind, Marie's husband looked at his wife and exclaimed, "Yes! Remember your first attempt at making Ravioli? They fell apart!" He laughed, as did Andréa, Marie's sister.

"When did that happen?" Alfredo asked. Marie frowned as she tried to recall. "Twenty years ago," she finally said. Intrigued, Mario asked, "Do you still make Ravioli?" "Yes, and they no longer fall apart." Marie's husband said, "Her Ravioli are great."

The conversation provided Alfredo and Mario with more lessons.

Ravioli Rule: Carry old Ravioli making memories to the table, but don't rub past mistakes in someone's face. Mistakes are positives: from these, learn and make better Ravioli.

One Sunday Uncle Vito and his boys came for dinner. Fortunately, Alfredo and Mario made extra Ravioli, for Vito's son, little Francesco, ate a copious amount. He finished one bowl then helped himself to a second. When he stopped to take a breath, he said, "Let's have some more!"

He had about five dishes and then didn't want to eat Ravioli again for about six months.

Another lesson learned.

Ravioli Rule: Don't overwhelm and burnout the dinner guests that they will never eat Ravioli again. Keep them wanting more. They'll keep coming back.

Another important lesson involved a Sunday dinner with Uncle Ralph's family. One of his four boys was reacting badly to Ravioli – an allergic reaction to the cheese, apparently. Father and brothers loudly enjoyed the one son's displeasure.

"What's wrong with him," Uncle Ralph laughed. "Maybe it's the Ravioli – or maybe it's just him!" said the amused brothers. Far more concerned, Alfredo and Mario offered the discomforted boy a meatball and traditional plain pasta.

Ravioli Rule: Sometimes, circumstances call for an alternative. Provide the option. Don't laugh at someone's discomfort; be compassionate about their needs. Respect is the key word. The fault is not with them or with you.

By this time, Alfredo and Mario had a lot of experience under their belts. They benefited from practice. Now, they faced their biggest test. Three of their relatives were coming over for dinner. It was a rough day. They weren't in the door for more than 10 minutes before they began arguing about the best way to make Ravioli. On and on the dispute raged – what kind of eggs should be used (large or extra large)? What kind of water is preferable (fresh from the spring or charcoal-cleaned and purified)? Where should the flour come from (South Dakota or Italy)?

Diplomatic—and ever wanting to learn more—the boys tried to make peace. "Tell us how you make your Ravioli," said Alfredo. "Yes, please, each of you," added Mario.

"Yes, we want to learn from each," said Alfredo. "Don't try and tell us who makes the best."

They thought it over and finally agreed that making the best Ravioli was a personal decision; you need to suit a person's taste. With peace at hand, the family members gained respect for these ambitious boys. Meanwhile, Alfredo and Mario were given an up-close lesson on how to handle disagreements. They gained a sense of how to turn a win-lose argument into a win-

win situation.

Again, they were ever learning.

Ravioli Rule: Learn to settle Ravioli-making disagreements by genuinely listening to both sides. Be open and objective. Understand the other's perspective. And remember –disagreeing doesn't mean being disagreeable.

One Saturday, when Alfredo and Mario prepared for yet another Sunday dinner, the boys found bugs in their flour. "How can this be," wailed Alfredo, the type who demanded answers – and now!

He began fretting about everything else. "Could bugs be in the Ravioli we already made?! Are they in all of our flour again!?" His pressed his palms against his temples. "Is everything ruined!?"

The more reasonable Mario tried to soothe him. "You're making a mountain out of a molehill. This is a small issue that we can overcome. It's easy to get more flour. We even have more in the cupboard. Check it out. Are the bugs in that flour? If so, then so what? We can buy more! We can get it together! Don't let it consume you!"

What Mario was trying to tell Alfredo is that you can't let surmountable distractions turn your focus away from the things that really need attention. Such distractions will only negatively impact the making of the Ravioli.

Ravioli Rule: Pay attention to both big and little errors. But don't be consumed by the smaller ones. Simply fix them. You could miss the larger errors that may boil to the surface. Indeed, the mistakes could boil over. You don't want to hear that kind of sizzle.

On another Sunday dinner, the boys were serving the Tamini family. When they arrived, the head of the family said, "We have been looking forward to eating the Ravioli from the moment we were invited."

Word was out; the boys were making Ravioli, and making them well. But for this latest dinner, Alfredo and Mario tried something different: They made two Ravioli types (meat and cheese).

Alfredo served the cheese Ravioli first. While the family ate these, the boys served the meat Ravioli. Their guests loudly voiced an odd complaint: "Why did you serve the cheese first? Are these your favorite? We are not stupid. We know you favor the meat!" "We just wanted to make two different Ravioli this time," the boys said, trying to calm the family down.

Things became a bit more complicated when other families heard that the Tamini's were served two types. "Why are they making one type for us and two for them," an offended member asked. "That doesn't seem fair!"

Alfredo and Mario heard all about this for several days. This episode proved another learning lesson. The next week, Alfredo and Mario made four different types of Ravioli, all with the same meat sauce. They brought them out on a large plate with four different sections. Comments were complimentary.

"What a presentation! What a delivery!" "You have four Ravioli on one dish. You must love them all!"

Ravioli Rule: If you serve one Ravioli type first, you may unintentionally give the perception that you favor one over another. Be fair to all the Ravioli.

As the boys moved forward in their Ravioli-making quest, each Sunday dinner provided them a new and unique learning experience. One Sunday, Uncle Primo came for a fourth time. Each time, the boys had made a different sauce: meat, pesto, white sauce and blush sauce.

This compelled Uncle Primo to ask: "Can't you make up your mind? Each time, you make a different sauce." With finger pointed in their faces, Uncle Primo strongly advised, "find one you like and stick with it." The boys explained that they were experimenting with different sauces. They didn't know that this would turn out to be such a big deal.

"Now I understand," said Uncle Primo, with a wide grin. "That makes sense! What's the sauce for next week?"

Ravioli Rule: When you serve different Ravioli sauce for people always expecting the same sauce, they will wonder about your intentions. Clearly explain your logic. You'll achieve buy-in, and people will believe in your efforts and become part of your Ravioli team.

On another Sunday, as Alfredo and Mario were spending hours preparing the Ravioli—making the dough, mixing the ricotta cheese, cooking the tomato sauce, adding the meat they prepared a day earlier—Aunt Prima (no relation to Uncle Primo) showed up and began talking about making the

Ravioli.

And she talked and talked – about the best way to make Ravioli and the best way to present the final product. Another relative overheard the conversation. She entered the kitchen and asked Aunt Prima, "Tell me how you make your fancy Italian bread?"

Aunt Prima answered the question—again at length—and this diverted her attention away from the boys, who could now finish making their Ravioli. Eventually, Aunt Prima occupied herself with making bread for the dinner.

Ravioli Rule: *Distractions get in the way of making Ravioli and need to be managed; otherwise distractions make the Ravioli process take forever. Distractions need to be diverted with another integral cooking project.*

The relatives that scared the boys the most were known as Aunt H and Uncle T (for "hurricane" and "tornado"). Their turbulent personalities were part of family legend, and now they were coming over for dinner. On past occasions, "Uncle Tornado" would arrive and be initially calm. Then someone would ask him a perfectly innocent question that would cause him to explode. Once, someone asked him which kind of egg was best for making dough (small, medium, large, extra large, jumbo?). Well, "Uncle Tornado" lived up to his name and tore through the room, voicing a loud diatribe about how best to use an egg. Aunt Hurricane was just a big storm. You knew the whirlwind was coming. You just needed to be prepared for the uncertain damage.

They were legends in the family and—gasp!—they were coming over for dinner. But the boys survived their encounter and learned another lesson.

Ravioli Rule: *You will always have to weather storms like "Aunt Hurricane" and "Uncle Tornado." There's no way around it. Maintain composure; do the best you can. Then stay behind and clean up the damage. That's how you make Ravioli through stormy weather.*

One weekend, Aunt Gabriela came over and watched the boys make the Ravioli. She was so proud. As she watched Alfredo and Mario dropped the Ravioli in the water, she wanted to celebrate. She uncorked a bottle of Dom Perignon and uncovered some appetizers and demanded the boys join her in a celebration of the Ravioli's immersion into the hot water.

Aunt Gabriela, Alfredo and Mario became so enwrapped in this celebration that food preparation suffered. The Ravioli were overcooked and too soft. When drained in the colander, they broke apart. There's an old saying, "A watched pot never boils." But the boys had taken their mind off of the pot, and their Ravioli was far less than "perfect." They had become overconfident.

Ravioli Rule: Celebrate Ravioli at the right time: when they are finished and ready to eat. A too-early celebration indicates overconfidence and complacency, which results in poor quality.

As the boys gained more experience, their reputation within the family grew. Relatives knew the boys were well organized. One Saturday, Alfredo and Mario were visited by as many as 12 relatives. They all wanted to offer their advice.

Make Ravioli with square edges, one said. Said another: "No, round!" "No! Here's how you do it," said yet one more relative, demonstrating how to make squares with fluted edges with a fork.

Another advised making agnolitti, or half-Raviolis. The kitchen debates went on and on, slowing down the boys' Ravioli-making process. So, Alfred and Mario agreed that they would minimize relatives' visits into their workspace. They'd only allow a small number of people in the kitchen. In the future, the boys enticed the meddlesome relatives out of the kitchen with some appetizers. Thus, they were able to continue their work unencumbered by too much extra input.

Ravioli Rule: Too many Ravioli managers in the kitchen spoil the Ravioli making.

By this time, Alfredo and Mario were becoming quite adept at handling perceived problems. They were absorbing their lessons well. However, things don't always proceed smoothly and, on one Ravioli-making day, they encountered the "full moon syndrome" – when everything seems to go wrong.

First, the gas stove didn't function. A temporary fix proved ineffective, as the main line had been broken. That breakage, in turn, impacted water pipelines. Water supply is crucial to cooking Ravioli. Next, the electricity went out. In their darkness, the boys realized they had no candles, which affected meal preparation and meal serving.

"What can happen next," Mario exclaimed. But the boys persisted. They even laughed about their compounding misfortunes. Ever resourceful, they borrowed candles from neighbors and even set up an outdoor fire, where they could keep all pots heated.

Against considerable odds, the boys made the Ravioli and served a meal. Their appreciative family gave them a standing ovation.

Ravioli Rule: Be persistent and resilient and never resigned to bad circumstances. Laugh in the face of adversity and you'll recover. Relatives, friends and co-Ravioli makers will admire how you overcome stress-filled obstacles. After you successfully make and serve the Ravioli, they may even share the laugh with you.

One day a relative said to the boys, "You make great Ravioli. In a month, my daughter will graduate. Would you be able to make your Ravioli for 150 people?" The boys first gulped. Then, they accepted this new challenge.

Ravioli Rule: Remain composed and positive when confronted with a new challenge. After all, you've been asked because you developed a reputation – you demonstrated skill and ability. Be ready to take the next step, even if your stomach churns with apprehension.

The boys needed to prepare one more Sunday dinner before the big holiday event. This one would include some neighbors. Neighbors had heard about the Sunday extravaganzas and jumped at the invitation.

The meal proved a success; neighbors loved the meal. They even asked for the recipe. Then came the momentous occasion, the boys served their Ravioli on white plates, with floral design around the edges. They avoided usage of blue plates. Alfredo and Mario remembered what several neighbors told them two years earlier: "I always hated when your family had dinner served on blue plates." Blue plates discolored the food's presentation.

So, Alfredo and Mario had listened, remembered and implemented. They knew what people preferred, and they integrated the feedback. This taught them yet one more important lesson: listen to the Ravioli eater, and then take the appropriate action.

Ravioli Rule: When you accommodate someone's preferences, you increase their comfort level. You make them feel welcome, important, and valuable and included in the meal preparation. You exceed expectations and create a solid relationship.

So the big family holiday event arrived. The boys had planned, made, cooked and served 1,000 Ravioli to family members – all done flawlessly. The Ravioli were perfect, the sauce savory. Some family members thanked the boys for the great job. Compliments flew from wall to wall. The boys smiled from ear to ear.

"Come to my house and cook anytime," one relative exclaimed. "Have your next dinner at my house," begged another, "and make meatballs, too!"

A well-satisfied and well-feed uncle embraced the boys in his hard thick arms and pulled them into his soft round belly. "You guys should open a restaurant!"

But the most interesting comments came from the relatives whose advice the boys earlier solicited during their basic learning phase. The aunt who criticized them most harshly ("They can't make Ravioli") took credit. Another uncle, whose help was equally ineffectual, said, "They came to my house, too, seeking advice."

Others realized the relatives tried to take credit where credit wasn't due, and they smiled tolerantly. Still others weren't willing to give any credit. In hypercritical whispers, they hissed, "this is the worst Ravioli I ever tasted."

Alfredo and Mario weren't deaf to the comments. "Not everyone feels that way," proclaimed Alfredo. Behind him, Mario nodded in agreement. "Maybe this was just a bad batch," one of the harshest family critics suggested.

"All the Ravioli were made the same way, on the same day, and at the same time," Alfredo defended. "Well! I never," said one indignant relative, who left the house in a huff, other family critics following close behind.

The boys reflected on this latest event. "I guess comments are going to be varied," said Alfredo to Mario.

His brother thought for a moment, then came up with a profound perception. "Feedback will be as mixed as the ingredients and the various rules," said Mario.

Alfredo's eyes widened. "That's good!" he said.

Ravioli Rule: Understand when to take credit and how to deal with criticism.

Ravioli menu:

■ Some people will take credit for your success when not due. But remember, smart people will realize whether credit is true or untrue.

■ True people will reward you for making outstanding Ravioli.

■ Those who don't are selfish or shortsighted. They like to feel better about themselves. Remember, your purpose is selfless and your vision is clear.

■ As far as criticism, never get angry, never seek to get even: Your best efforts will stand out in the end. Just do your work, make great Ravioli unencumbered by the insecurity of others.

Alfredo and Mario moved from small functions, like family events, and opened their own Ravioli business.

RAVIOLI - THE MANAGING

Open a Ravioli business and manage people

The Ravioli big family holiday dinners proved successful, and family members started asking the boys to make Ravioli for weddings, christenings and other important occasions. In six months, almost every family party featured Alfredo and Mario's Ravioli. In one year, they catered 45 different dinners, almost one per week. Why not go into business, the boys thought. They would gather knowledge and experience from others, just as they did in their initial Ravioli-making phase.

They went to more than 20 restaurants, to watch how the Ravioli were made and presented. They also observed the management process. In each restaurant, they befriended the staff, so they could ask questions. Waiters let them into the kitchens, where they watched how the cooks made Ravioli. They were keen observers; they absorbed the good and the bad from each restaurant.

They believed if they learned from the best and improved on it, they would benefit. They wanted to be world class, even set new standards. They chose role models carefully and expanded on examples. Conversely, they learned what irritated customers, so as not to repeat mistakes. They viewed mistakes as learning opportunities. From the weakness of others, they would gain strength.

The process took about five months. The next big recipe was a business plan. This took their rules to the next level, and experience proved the best teacher.

First, they started a small catering business, a two-man operation. As their business grew, they hired help. With this development, they became managers – managing the efforts of Ravioli makers.

Ravioli Rule: *Learn the Ravioli making process from seasoned and well-experienced Ravioli makers. If you don't learn from other people's experiences, then it is called the dope and dopie Ravioli making approach. If you don't learn from Other People's Experiences then you become a Dope; if you Don't learn from Other People's Intelligent Experiences then you become Dopie. The intelligent experiences allow you to learn, grow and improve on those experiences, as if you almost experienced it yourself.*

Alfredo and Mario recognized the need for more assistance in making the Ravioli. Business would mean more than just the two of them making the Ravioli – cooking, making the sauce and completing the presentation. At times, they were overwhelmed. What would happen if one were to fall ill? They needed a backup plan. Demand exceeded supply and work exceeded their capacity.

They sought help. Surprisingly, 75 people showed up. The boys turned away all but ten. Five would make the Ravioli; the other five would organize the preparation and inventory room.

After about a week there was too much inventory in the room. They had large supplies of flour, water and eggs. The processing of Ravioli was a little slower than expected. So, Alfredo and Mario had the inventory people assist in making the Ravioli and had only a few others help in the preparation, planning and cleanup.

In the process of educating people on how to make Ravioli, the boys established an educational seminar for the new Ravioli makers, which included hands-on experience. First, these students watched Alfredo and Mario and then worked side by side. Finally, they made Ravioli on their own, guided by the boys. Once their education was completed, the students were awarded a certificate of genuine "Ravioli Makers," which meant that they were more than just employees.

Some of the new Ravioli makers decided that they knew how to make the Ravioli best and started playing and looked for shortcuts like breaking eggs the day before, or letting the flour sit out, which dried it out and affected the liquid-to-flour ratio. The result was poor quality Ravioli. This upset cus-

tomers and impacted repeat business. Shortcuts didn't work, Alfredo and Mario realized. They stopped it before it negatively impacted the integrity and quality of their Ravioli.

Ravioli Rule: *Always make the Ravioli right. Payoff will be long term. Shortcuts can damage quality.*

Several of Alfredo and Mario's Ravioli makers made Ravioli well– they shared the same thoughts, commitment and dedication about the process. Ravioli was their passion. Alfredo and Mario decided to let them manage the process. The Ravioli they made was high quality, and the dinners they managed went off without a hitch. The Ravioli business was on autopilot with a core group of people managing the process.

Ravioli Rule: *Give Ravioli makers who demonstrate initiative and understanding more responsibility, either independently or collectively. When they are successful, you can let them be the Ravioli managers and trust them.*

When Alfredo and Mario showed the new students how to make the Ravioli, they explained the details. For instance, they made sure that they understood the ricotta cheese should not overfill the dough pockets – because the cheese would expand in the dough pocket while in the boiling water and, therefore, rupture the entire Ravioli. Alfredo and Mario wanted to make sure these Ravioli makers knew and understood the reasons behind making the right decisions.

Ravioli Rule: *When you make clear the rationale of why you do something to or for the Ravioli, the makers will understand. They will give you their full backing and sell the logic to future Ravioli makers.*

Alfredo and Mario made the Ravioli with such enthusiasm that it inspired the students and made them even more excited. Alfredo and Mario agreed with the students' perception. "Anytime you make Ravioli, it should feel like the first time," said Alfredo.

"Otherwise, you are going to rest on your laurels," added Mario. "That's a recipe for failure, not success." "Complacency breeds decreased quality," continued Alfredo.

Ravioli Rule: *Make every Ravioli-making event as exciting as the first. You will succeed if you have the same attitude and excitement that you had when you made your first Ravioli.*

Whenever Alfredo and Mario got together to make or talk about Ravioli, they generated a lot of interest. People—including the Ravioli-making students, townspeople and family members—watched every move they made. The boys were taken aback by the close attention. One of the new students explained it for them: "I like watching you because I learn," he said. "I know that you are the best, so I could become even better."

Alfredo and Mario realized that what they did—their slightest move—profoundly affected many people. They were setting an example. They were creating their legacy. They agreed to meet the high expectations, as those who watched would become better Ravioli makers.

Ravioli Rule: People watch because they want to be like you. Just as you learned from the best, new Ravioli makers want to watch and learn from you. So be the best, and then they will be even better, and you will significantly affect the next generation of Ravioli makers.

One day the new students were making Ravioli and sauce. The Ravioli were placed in the boiling water and cooked al dente. When one of the students sampled the Ravioli, it tasted starchy. Either there was not enough water in the pot, or the dough went flat, or the ricotta cheese was turning sour. One of the students thought if he applied one of the better sauces, it would camouflage the taste. Other students liked the idea. But when Alfredo and Mario tasted the result, their reaction was vehement: they spit it out. They quickly called a meeting of all students and firmly spoke about lack of quality. Don't ever compromise quality, they said. Ever!

Ravioli Rule: Bad Ravioli sticks like too much pasta cooked in not enough water. The cost of not replacing the Ravioli when it has lost its quality is too high. It amounts to loss of reputation. You need to know when it is time to remove the bad Ravioli and start over. There is a saying: there is never enough time to make the Ravioli right the first time but always enough time to make the Ravioli right the second time.

Alfredo and Mario were very busy, selling Ravioli and catering to several families in the neighborhood for weddings, graduations and even for some restaurants. They became so busy that they were not in the Ravioli shop.

This led the new Ravioli makers to resent them. They thought that Alfredo and Mario were out playing golf, eating, or looking for new Ravioli people, or—most disturbing—that Alfredo and Mario were not interested in their work. So work slowed down. Daily production dropped off.

One day, when Alfredo and Mario visited their shop, they perceived the resentment. One student gathered the courage to express the shared frustration. After that conversation, Alfredo and Mario decided to spend more time in the shop. The decision raised morale and made the team know that their daily work routine was important.

The boys not only spent more time in their shop. They held team lunches, where questions were raised and answers provided – about making pasta, experience, and the best and worst Ravioli. These lunches proved a significant organizational improvement. They strengthened the team, and the Ravioli makers took the messages home to their families. Alfredo and Mario, who were no longer boys but men with families of their own, decided to share the stories with their own children. Even the youngest became excited about making Ravioli.

Everyday Alfredo and Mario would hear about some child asking their parent, "How was the Ravioli today? Tell us how it turned out? Can we make Ravioli at home one day? Can you show us how you make the Ravioli?!"

These informal stories were great educational and learning tools for the children and gave them a step up, raising them to a higher vantage point, compared to other families who did not share Ravioli experiences.

After several months of these meetings, one of the young Ravioli makers thanked Alfredo and Mario for sharing their experience. He said that he kept notes on the most important messages. "I read these notes once a week and find ways to put them into action and build upon them," he added. "They supplement what I learn."

Alfredo and Mario realized that it is important to share and listen. "There are two sides to Ravioli making communication," observed Alfredo. Mario nodded. "One side involves sharing. The other side is listening and then acting on the gained knowledge."

Ravioli Rule: Be there when the Ravioli is made – and be attentive, observe. It is a strong message of support and interest that you care about the quality of the Ravioli and its makers. Give the people you work with and your children a step up by sharing your experience and knowledge. The smart Ravioli manager shares wisdom; the smarter Ravioli maker hears, listens and learns.

Alfredo and Mario were teaching the Ravioli making rules to several students. Some were grasping the concept and the process the first time around by listening to the theory and reading the preparation manual. For others, this learning process took longer. They had to repeat several steps and actually experience the Ravioli making technique.

Alfredo and Mario thought that people should learn quicker. They were holding the slow learning process against them and first judged they were not "the better" Ravioli makers. But as time passed, it turned out that the slower-learning Ravioli students actually made Ravioli quicker and with better quality than those who excelled in the class. Alfredo and Mario realized that you should not hold the learning experience against someone, particularly those that didn't immediately grasp the process. Some may be slower, but once they see, they will understand and make the Ravioli very well.

Alfredo and Mario were very patient with such students. Some that experienced the Ravioli making process became the best makers. It took them longer; they just needed to visualize. One of the students, who needed to first experience the Ravioli making process, later opened his own restaurant in a neighboring town and did incredible business. It became known as the little Alfredo and Mario friendly rival Ravioli company.

Ravioli Rule: Some Ravioli makers will understand with simple guidance and direction. Others will need more attention and instruction. Others will even need the experience. Be patient with all. It will be worthwhile. They can become the best Ravioli makers.

During the making of the Ravioli one of the boys asked his fellow students, "Why do we use ricotta cheese? Why don't we use cottage cheese?" One of the boys said, "Because Alfredo and Mario have always done it that way, they have the experience, they know what is best." Another boy said, "Shut up, do your work and stop asking questions."

Alfredo and Mario now entered the room and said, "What is going on?" One boy stood up. "Someone was questioning why you use the ricotta cheese instead of cottage cheese and I told them that because it's the right thing to do. The both of you have the experience and you know what is right." "You're partially right," said Alfredo. "Who asked the question," said Mario. An embarrassed boy stood. He feared he was in trouble.

"Don't be afraid, son," said Alfredo. "You have the right to ask questions," said Mario. "You asked a good question. And the more you ask, the more you'll learn."

Alfredo and Mario then explained the reason they use ricotta cheese. Compared to cottage cheese, it's less lumpy and has better quality. Ricotta cheese is smoother and tastes better. "Also, we learned at a young age that if our aunt did not tell us the reason why something was done in making the Ravioli, we didn't learn and understand," Alfredo pointed out. "It raises your overall understanding when you understand the reason why. I am glad you asked the question."

The boy thanked him and said, "Now that I understand, I think we can add some new ingredients to the ricotta cheese. I don't think we could add it if it was cottage cheese."

"Explain," said Alfredo.

"We could add some new ingredients, such as a mushroom filling, some prosciutto, pesto and some ham and some chicken," said the boy, about his ideas. "It is almost like a takeoff from a calzone."

Alfredo and Mario looked at each other. "That's a good idea," said Alfredo. "Let's do it," exclaimed Mario.

Ravioli Rule: *The Ravioli maker who asks questions has an open, learning, creative and innovative Ravioli-making mind. Allow such a mind to rise just like yeast in bread dough.*

The Ravioli makers always used the Ravioli cutter that came from Italy. They had only 20 of them. It was a round device made of stainless steel and it made the impression on the Ravioli that cut the dough just right. The cutter actually made six small Ravioli. One day, the cutter got stuck in the machine and was bent beyond repair. Eventually, this happened to all twenty of them (the cutters were left on top of the pasta machines and reacted to the vibration of the pasta rollers and fell into the machine). The students were distraught about the delay in Ravioli making. One of the boys became irate. He stormed around screaming until he wore himself out. Another student calmed him down. "We can find our way out of this," he said. "Nothing is impossible until we can find the answer."

This, he did. He found drinking glasses and turned them upside down. The glasses were the same size as the Ravioli cutters. He took six, fastened them with a plastic device, and used this makeshift tool to produce the Ravioli until the replacement cutters arrived. He was thinking outside of the box. True, the process was slowed down, but the students found the first work-around when the systems are down, and they stayed calm, awaiting the arrival of the new Ravioli cutters.

Ravioli Rule: Nothing is impossible. And answers can be found. Stay calm during crisis. There is always a Ravioli work-around if something goes wrong.

One of the new cooks made horribly bad Ravioli. His sauce stuck to the bottom of the pot and burned. He forgot to stir the sauce and taste it. His colleagues wanted to throw him out of the class.

When told of the situation, Alfredo and Mario were far more tolerant. "Look, we all make mistakes," Alfredo told the students. "That's why failure is such a powerful learning tool. We learn from mistakes."

"That's part of our job," added Mario. Alfredo reminded them, "You made mistakes, too, when you first started. Remember when the pasta stuck to each other because there was too much pasta for the water. So, let's not hold this against him."

Ravioli Rule: If new Ravioli makers make a mistake, don't damn them to Ravioli hell. Everyone makes mistakes, and mistakes are opportunities for learning.

Alfredo and Mario were holding their educational instruction and had students from different parts of Italy. They were on loan for the summer and the parties were starting to heat up. So Alfredo and Mario showed them the way they make their Ravioli. The future Ravioli makers scratched their heads. "What type of Ravioli is this?"

During Alfredo and Mario's question-and-answer session, the Italian students learned about different types of Ravioli. The northerners call their Ravioli agnoletti, which are cut in half like a crescent moon shape. They were not round Ravioli. Those from other areas made square Ravioli and put ridges on the ends.

This was another learning experience: Ravioli means different things to different people of Italy. The students broadened their knowledge, expanded the menu and learned that there isn't always a specific way to make the right Ravioli. People from different regions have different perceptions.

Ravioli Rule: There are various ways to make Ravioli. Different regions of Italy make different Ravioli. When you tell an experienced Ravioli maker that there is only one way to make the Ravioli, it demeans their experience. It restrains their originality and resourcefulness. YOU can learn from an experienced Ravioli maker, too.

One day, Alfredo and Mario walked into the shop and were startled by what they saw. Eggs on the wall, flour on the floor, ricotta cheese spread out on all the appliances.

"What happened?!" "The machine whipping the ricotta cheese opened up and rotated all the cheese throughout the room," a student answered. "What about the eggs on the wall," asked Alfredo? "We slipped on the cheese and the eggs we carried spun out and hit the wall."

"How did the flour get on the floor?" "When we slipped, we also fell on the bags of flour and knocked them over." "Well, this was an interesting day," said Mario. "This never happened before."

Alfredo and Mario glanced at each other. Something just doesn't seem right. The situation smelled sour. "Well, we would have to investigate it further, maybe we could watch it on the videotape," said Mario. All the students looked at each in horror. They realized that their story would not hold up to the videotaped evidence. It had been fabricated.

Ravioli Rule: If something goes wrong and your senses and your gut says the tomato sauce has become acidic and the Ravioli smells sour, like ricotta cheese gone bad, then you should check if your instincts are right.

One group of students were excellent. They were meticulous about making the pasta, the Ravioli, and the ricotta cheese. They were slow and methodical, but their product was excellent. Alfredo and Mario liked the quality: the dough was elastic and the ricotta cheese was smooth, no Ravioli broke apart in the boiling water, and the sauce was excellent. Even the edges of the dough were perfect. When Alfredo and Mario asked them how they made the Ravioli so perfect, they said, "We made it the right way, we just paid attention to everything we did. We were focused. It wasn't attractive or dramatic. We just worked with the details and the job got done."

It paid off in excellent Ravioli.

Ravioli Rule: *Don't risk quality by rushing the Ravioli. Ravioli made the right way is worth the extra effort.*

During the years, the Ravioli machine had changed. When Alfredo and Mario saw the new contraption in action, they decided to buy it. The new machine was state of the art and pointed to the future. The new Ravioli makers were familiar with the new technology. It was efficient and offered the same quality as homemade Ravioli.

During a lull, when people were on break, Alfredo and Mario investigated how to make Ravioli with this new machine. It took them a while to get acclimated. Some of the students even wondered how Alfredo and Mario ever made Ravioli in their lives when they couldn't figure out this machine. Anyway, they finally got the hang of it and practiced and practiced, and before you knew it, these quick learners were making Ravioli the new way. All of the students applauded. Alfredo and Mario took a bow.

Ravioli Rule: *When the Ravioli machine has changed, you need to change, too, and learn how to use it.*

This incident was similar to a previous one. A student felt that as they were making the Ravioli, Alfredo and Mario (now managing this operation) were too far from the center of action. This student suggested that Alfredo and Mario be in the operation 24 hours a day.

So he approached Alfredo and Mario and the decision was very simple, they would stay in touch and in tune with the Ravioli making process. They would even make the Ravioli one day a month. Alfredo and Mario thought it was important to let the workers see that Ravioli making was important to them. It was good for Alfredo and Mario to stay in touch and stay fresh with the process, but they were not going to do the workers' work 24 hours a day. They needed to manage the business side now.

Ravioli Rule: *Just because you became the head chef doesn't mean you still can't make the Ravioli.*

One day, little Guido was helping make the Ravioli. It was his second day and he made several mistakes. He missed adding one egg to the egg/flour mixture. He used regular flour instead of semolina. He forgot the egg wash. The pasta wasn't secured and it broke apart. A bad day.

Little Guido felt he failed in his Ravioli-making quest. Alfredo and Mario took him under their wings. They pointed out his mistakes, but didn't mean to criticize; they only wanted to provide positive feedback. Alfredo and Mario outlined the steps, one by one, and showed Guido that he owned the Ravioli making process – what goes right and wrong. Little Guido understood. During this discussion, Alfredo and Mario expressed gratitude. Guido wanted to make the Ravioli, and they thanked him for his significant contribution. Little Guido understood the feedback and the positive message. From that point, he began making great Ravioli.

Ravioli Rule: *If a Ravioli maker messes up when making the Ravioli, make sure they understand they own the job and that Ravioli should be made correctly. End result: the Ravioli manager has groomed a better Ravioli maker, one that could become a Ravioli manager.*

Both Little Guido and Tomasino worked in the kitchen, and each were different as far as approach. Guido listened and understood direction given. Tomasino was different. He was independent-minded. Even by his fifth time at making Ravioli, he remembered the guidance, but he defied or forgot what he was taught. The patient Guido learned—and recovered—from his errors. The defiant Tomasino struggled. Alfredo and Mario remained patient and gave him attention, direction and experience. However, after subsequent failures, Alfredo and Mario made a decision: Tomasino wasn't a Ravioli maker. His talents resided elsewhere.

Ravioli Rule: *Provide learning opportunities, but recognize when it is time to let go. Not everyone will be a successful Ravioli maker. They have talents that reside elsewhere. When you let them go, tell them you believe in their skills – but also let them know they need to find a more suitable direction, for the benefit of both parties. It is an honest approach, and it will also reduce risk to your reputation.*

One day, Alfredo and Mario were working with one of the teams of five who had learned how to make the Ravioli. Guiseppe and Giovanni were the two best. They placed Guiseppe in charge of the weekend Ravioli-making team.

Giovanni was upset and ready to express grief. But he possessed inherent leadership skills, so he kept quiet. True, he felt upset about not being consulted—and in how the decision was communicated to him—but his patient attitude paid off. As time went on, Alfredo and Mario realized that Giovanni was the better choice to manage the weekend team. If Giovanni had first screamed and shouted, this opportunity would have been unavailable. Indeed, Giovanni demonstrated great poise in a difficult situation, which Alfredo and Mario recognized. The reward: a management position.

Ravioli Rule: Good Ravioli managers understand when and when not to be in charge of managing the Ravioli makers. Being ready, reliable and patient define the profile of Ravioli makers that will ultimately get their turn.

Alfredo and Mario were walking under the floor in the foundation area when they overheard the new Ravioli makers above them making nice comments.

"I enjoy working for these brothers," one said. "Yes, I do too," said another. "Indeed," said the youngest of the lot. "They take interest in not just the product, but in us. They listen. I believe that my opinions are heard."

Another learning experience for Alfredo and Mario – it increased the dedication to making the Ravioli.

Ravioli Rule: Let Ravioli makers know you are open and appreciate their thoughts and opinions, and be authentic about the request – it goes a long way in satisfying the new Ravioli makers.

Alfredo and Mario hired the next group of people to help them make the Ravioli. All of them answered "yes" to the basic question – had they made Ravioli before?

This set expectations higher and accelerated the new class. But problems became apparent: When a new student, Roberto, made his Ravioli, it was painfully evident that he was inexperienced. Classmates were embarrassed for him when he asked questions such as "How many eggs do I use? How much flour is required for Ravioli?" Classmates weren't just embarrassed; they were angered: Obviously Roberto lied about his credentials. What else would he lie about?! He no longer had any credibility.

Alfredo and Mario were getting verbal communications that Roberto slowed everyone down. The quality of the class was not up to speed. So Alfredo and Mario kindly asked him for a private meeting.

"What's your Ravioli making experience," asked Alfredo, not harshly. "How were you taught to make Ravioli," asked Mario. "We've never seen your technique before."

Alfredo and Mario didn't want to turn the situation into an interrogation. Rather, they pushed forward gently but intently. Indeed, Alfredo was curious. "Did you learn it from a different part of Italy?"

Roberto looked from man to man.

Mario continued. "We've learned about different types of Ravioli and Ravioli making in different parts of Italy." His gaze was a bit more intense than Alfredo's. "Who showed you how to make Ravioli?"

Roberto answered: "I learned a long time ago, from a friend, but I can't remember the exact lessons." Alfredo and Mario looked at each other with knowing glances. Still, they continued. "Who was this person," asked Alfredo. "Give me a moment, I'll remember the time, the person," stuttered Roberto.

Alfredo sighed and looked down at the table, and then at Mario, who nodded. They knew they were confronting a liar. The decision was immediately made: Roberto was gone. Alfredo and Mario conducted their business with the highest level of integrity and expected all partners and associates to be truthful.

Ravioli Rule: Great Ravioli makers and managers have integrity and don't exaggerate or fabricate their abilities. Others will know the difference and you will lose credibility. As a Ravioli manager, you need to find ways to filter fact from fiction.

One day, Alfredo and Mario walked into the kitchen and watched the new students make Ravioli. But Alfredo and Mario didn't like the way some of the boys rolled the dough. One kneaded the dough from right to left, and then kneaded it from left to right. Another student kneaded it from top to bottom. Yet another did it from bottom to top.

"Consistency!" shouted Alfredo. The students looked at him. "It should all be done in the same way," Mario told the fearful students.

One person placed the ricotta cheese from the far end to the near end. Alfredo and Mario thought you should do the near end first. They watched the team and offered advice on every detail.

Managing minutia is important, but it annoyed the students. They felt they were getting lost in technical details and were being second-guessed by Alfredo and Mario, who criticized students for not seeing the big picture. Students felt they weren't recognized as adults. They felt that everything they did was believed to be wrong, and that management had no faith in their abilities. They were dispirited.

"Have faith in us," said a brave new student. "We know what we're doing!"

Ravioli Rule: *Never micromanage. Ravioli managers should establish the right recipe. From there, let the new Ravioli makers learn how to handle the details. They don't need to be lectured on how to boil water.*

In new education sessions, Alfredo and Mario relaxed a bit – a relief to students who felt their teachers were too stiff. They brought joviality into the classroom. When they started to make the Ravioli, Alfredo and Mario juggled the eggs and tossed them at each other like circus clowns, a way to bring a little excitement and fun in the pasta making process. They even told jokes and laughed at their own stories.

They later discovered these students took that impression of humor and egg juggling, and after their education, started juggling eggs during the daily work efforts. Alfredo and Mario watched the impact of their labors deteriorate because of this humorous approach. Students didn't take their responsibilities seriously; therefore, Ravioli making wasn't taken seriously. It got to the point that the original students, taught under the serious mode, were in conflict with the students that subscribed to the humorous approach.

One new student said, "This is the new way Alfredo and Mario taught us. Get in step with today's Ravioli." Older students responded, "That is not how we were taught." So, some of the boys continued to throw eggs in the air. It became contagious.

Ravioli Rule: *If you are the head Ravioli manager, think twice about when and how you act. Your thoughts and actions make strong impressions on the young Ravioli makers. They'll mimic your actions, so demonstrate the right way to behave and be consistent.*

Alfredo and Mario needed to prepare for a very large party. Now very knowledgeable about human behavior, they prepared for this event by motivating Ravioli makers. They entertained an option: bringing in a set of temporary people. But quality and efficiency could be lost with this approach. So they called all Ravioli makers to a special meeting and said they have a large gathering in two weeks and needed to get extra efforts from them starting next week. Everyone would need to work harder, faster, at longer hours, and maintain quality. They'd get paid for it, but it would only be a one- to two-week event. They laid out the reasons why they would not be hiring temporary people, and they explained why they needed their current Ravioli makers' expertise and skills.

Alfredo confronted the class and said, "This effort is critically important, because when we are successful the good news will spread to others." Mario raised a finger. "But if we err, that news will spread even quicker."

The Ravioli makers understood the importance of prioritizing extra effort. The next week they surprised Alfredo and Mario and finished one day ahead of schedule.

Ravioli Rule: Ravioli making entails strong managerial skills. Ravioli managers need to know how to get extraordinary efforts from the Ravioli makers. Extraordinary effort is given when asked. Just don't ask for extraordinary effort every second because then it becomes routine.

Something similar happened two weeks later. They had to make 5,000 Ravioli and knew they didn't have the resources to complete the tasks. So they got a list of other people recommended from the Ravioli makers. Alfredo and Mario interviewed them and gave them an accelerated education on Ravioli making. They explained the necessary preparations. Alfredo and Mario also advised them that there was not an opportunity for them to work permanently. However, if they did well this next week, and if the Ravioli making business continues to do well and expand, they would keep their names on file for future opportunities. So, with a handful of new people, after being educated on the Ravioli making process, they made the Ravioli—all 5,000—and perfectly. Beaming with happiness, Alfredo and Mario rewarded the overachievement.

Ravioli Rule: You can get incredible results from everyday people who possess no experience, provided they have the right attitude. Just give them the education, tools, values and inspiration.

One day some of the new students watched as Alfredo and Mario made the Ravioli, and they were fascinated by the love in the brothers' eyes. Alfredo and Mario held each Ravioli as if it was a baby.

"Why do you still love Ravioli, after so many years," a student asked. "Ravioli are our children," answered Alfredo.

Mario expanded on this idea: "Every parent sees a child as an investment. Not a financial investment, but an investment into the future of the world. We do the best we can to nurture that investment. We offer care. We want success. We want all to be successful. So it is with Ravioli, which we nurture from the beginning, from the dough making to the completion."

Ravioli Rule: Treat the Ravioli as if you are a parent. Care for it. Nurture it. Ultimately, you want the Ravioli to be successful.

One day, one Ravioli manager talked up a storm. "She never shuts up," one student whispered to another. "Yes," whispered the other. "She constantly talks about herself, and her mother's villa in Tuscany, and her father's teaching position, and how proud she is of her five brothers."

Another student overheard the conversation and interjected, "She tells everyone all the details of her life. She doesn't stop." "That's right," said one more student. "She doesn't let others talk. During conversations, she constantly interrupts, which makes people uncomfortable." "And she laughs at her own jokes, which aren't even funny," said another.

One more student offered this observation: "It's not that the jokes aren't funny, they are sarcastic. Her barbs hurt people." This person they spoke of had no respect for the Ravioli and, more importantly, the Ravioli makers.

Alfredo and Mario became apprised of the situation and took the offensive student aside. "If you can't respect Ravioli and fellow Ravioli makers, then you need to go somewhere else," Mario told her, in a private conversation.

She went elsewhere.

Ravioli Rule: Learn respect – of the Ravioli and its makers. Only talk when your words contribute to the process.

Alfredo and Mario's pasta business continued growing. They catered several dozen events each week. They chose one of the superior Ravioli makers who had been with them for two years. They relied on him. He was the technician who knew all the details. He lived with the day-to-day operations. He would be their chief Ravioli maker. One day, he advised them they should create a count of daily production. There should be a count of inventory received and used, total Ravioli made and the number of people to make Ravioli. Separately, there should be a catering event count to indicate the number of events, guests at each event and the number of Ravioli people that worked the event.

This would create a tracking system that would help anticipate needed resources in materials and people, and the amount of Ravioli made or sold on a daily and per event basis. The tracking of this information would also highlight the high and low days and events of the year. Alfredo and Mario liked this idea. They started a tracking system.

Ravioli Rule: Listen to the head chef and the Ravioli manager, especially if you are out of touch and the head chef and Ravioli manager are closer to the details. A Ravioli tracking system will enable Ravioli managers to pay attention to the details, identify weaknesses, focus their attention, and provide a good historical reference to project future volume.

One day, Alfredo and Mario noticed the inventory of Ravioli and meatballs were dwindling. They came up about five pounds short of their 100-pound inventory. They kept excellent records, but one weekend—before a holiday—they discovered they were 10 pounds short.

"What happened to the Ravioli," Alfredo asked some workers. One of the workers said they thought someone was stealing the Ravioli and meatballs. So Alfredo and Mario installed cameras to monitor activity. The cameras caught the culprits. They were fired. Theft decreased their credibility. What else were they doing?

This episode made Alfredo and Mario more aware about the relationships they had with customers. They checked the files and there were a handful of complaints, but only at the events worked by these two individuals. It was only about three pounds of Ravioli missing at each event. So they contacted these customers and offered about five pounds of Ravioli, meatballs and sausage as compensation. They wanted to go above and beyond to build credibility. Future relationships and friendships were at stake.

Ravioli Rule: Ravioli managers need Ravioli makers with integrity. You need to go above and beyond when you have erred, even if the customers are unaware of the error. It will make you and your enterprise more credible.

The catering business was expanding. A huge event loomed. About 1,000 people needed to be served. The business needed to make more than 7,500 Ravioli and 5,000 meatballs and sausage, as well as to bake bread, serve wine and provide all of the dishes, utensils and napkins. And as it was the biggest event yet so far, the company needed to provide tents. Planning went on for weeks – and this included outlining tent locations, the Ravioli volume, the amount of sauce and meatballs. The staff also needed to keep everything fresh. Logistics were complex.

It was a massive job, the biggest in Ravioli history. It was well planned, well executed; all went perfectly. Alfredo and Mario were so happy they gave their crew a specially created Ravioli paper certificate of commendation immediately after the event. Even group photos were taken; the pictures were filled with hugs. The successful event created a bond of unity. Staff beamed with pride at the recognition. It put the icing on the cake – or the sauce on the Ravioli!

Ravioli Rule: When you thank the Ravioli makers for doing a world-class job for a special event, do it immediately. It indicates you were so impressed you didn't need to think about or wait for the recognition process.

The business kept growing. It catered weddings and supplied restaurants.

One day, while Mario was out of town managing a wedding, Alfredo hurt his back. Fortunately, Alfredo had been mentoring a student named Vito. Alfredo had given Vito excellent directions and coached him through a successful Ravioli making process. He also had great experience because he also practiced managing the Ravioli makers. Alfredo relied on him to make the Ravioli from beginning to end. So Alfredo asked Vito, "Manage the business for this one day, while I recover. I will provide you with the goals and objectives."

The process ran smoothly and the Ravioli were made perfectly as if Alfredo was here. The next day Alfredo tasted a sample of the Ravioli delivered to one of the restaurants. It was superb. He shared a bottle of Vino Nobile with the team and gave credit to Vito. He never mentioned that one of the reasons they were successful was because of the early education, mentoring and transition strategy he (Alfredo) put in place.

Ravioli Rule: When great Ravioli managers are absent, they have already established well-organized plans and practice sessions for the team to smoothly manage the Ravioli making process.

Ravioli menu:

- A great Ravioli manager provides the right tools, values and education to the team. Let members practice making the Ravioli as if there are no managers. As a result, on days when the Ravioli managers are out, the team will pull through since they are on autopilot.

- Selfish Ravioli managers allow the Ravioli making process to appear flawed while they are away to make themselves look good.

- Ravioli managers must thank the Ravioli makers and not get too absorbed in leadership skills for letting them practice.

- Thank the Ravioli makers, whether or not they worked directly for you. Give recognition liberally and realistically, and create friends. The authentic celebration could come in handy for long-term support, collaboration, and teamwork.

During a team meeting, a new student, who wanted to be a master Ravioli maker, but who was overwhelmed with the work, asked, "What should come first – the dishes, the table dressing, the pasta or the meatballs?"

The new and excited manager, Isabella, blurted out, "Everything is a priority!" The answer confused the team, resulting in bickering among the young Ravioli makers, the meatball makers and the people that manage the table settings.

Everyone got in everybody's way. The result was less than spectacular. The statement that "everything is a priority" stressed all of them so that the balance of what came first and second was off. Timing was off. Pasta was good, of course, but the making of it was inefficient and unproductive. Meatballs were presented before the pasta was served.

The wrong perception and tone were set because the expectations weren't clearly defined. Alfredo and Mario told Isabella that, "everything can't be a priority because less important things may get done first and the Ravioli will get lost in the mix."

Ravioli Rule: *Telling the Ravioli makers that everything is a priority will confuse them and disrupt the process flow. Some parts need to be finished before you start on another part.*

Alfredo and Mario decided they wanted to do something different to their Ravioli. There were already different shapes: agnolitti, half moon, tortellini, tortelloni, square and round. Now, they wanted to try their own, to put their individual stamp on the Ravioli. So, they tried different type oversized Ravioli and even mini Ravioli. What finely worked was large-sized tortelloni. They became the only Ravioli makers to produce this type of pasta. It created for them a new niche. Restaurants were ordering. Creativity worked.

Ravioli Rule: After you learn how to make the Ravioli, be innovative, think outside of the square and the round Ravioli. Put your signature on the Ravioli.

Making Ravioli in machines was a task that required a lot of attention. Once, while a team was making the Ravioli, the machine stopped. They thought it was a hairpin from Maria's hairnet that fell on the rolling bins and stopped the machine. This event almost triggered a catastrophe.

The machine stopped everyone; all the other Ravioli machines stopped because people wondered what happened.

"What's going on," yelled the floor manager. "We think a hairpin got stuck in the machine," explained a team member. This provoked laughter from other teams. Fingers were pointed, and one team denigrated another team's capabilities.

"They probably put too much flour in the recipe and everything got stuck," said a member of one team. "They could never make the Ravioli right!" Another team leader said, "They've always been the weak link." But another person recognized the real problem. A large screw fell off the metal supports above and into the pasta machine, causing it to stop.

At this point, Alfredo and Mario stepped in. They heard about this Ravioli rumor and met with the teams individually and raised with them their level of professionalism. "Unless the facts are known, no one should speculate or accuse," stressed Alfredo. "Don't judge anyone or make a decision until facts are known."

Ravioli Rule: Your perspective depends on alignment and position point to witness what really happened. When making a decision, be properly aligned. Facts speak the truth. Learn everyone's perspective, understand their reflection.

During a catering event, a new manager was publicly thanked for putting together a great evening. Food was delicious, tables set meticulously and wine was perfect. Francesco, the new manager, felt gratified. "Everything was perfect," he asked.

Not really, a guest said: "There was one problem. Some of the chairs were wet from the earlier rain. When we sat, our clothes got wet."

"I am so sorry," Francesco said. "It must have been someone else. Maybe Vito or Roberto."

Alfredo and Mario heard this story and added a new educational segment to the program, ensuring that everyone should know how to take a big kiss but also know how to take a punch. Don't deflect the punch and take only the kiss.

Ravioli Rule: When you are thanked and you take all the credit for making the Ravioli, stand up and take responsibility for any failure that occurred.

Gino was one person who never assumed the responsibility when something went wrong. He was always ready with an excuse and to point blame.

"Don't look at me" was his Ravioli-making mantra. But this statement flew in the face of evidence. The day the flour spilled on the floor, everyone saw him do it. Everyone knew it was him. Television monitors don't lie, and Alfredo and Gino watched the videotaped evidence. They took Gino aside, and advised him that he should get more serious about his work. Further, they advised Gino that blaming others leads to loss of credibility and respect.

So, assume responsibility for anything that goes wrong within a facility, even if you weren't responsible. It happened on your watch.

Coaching Gino, Alfredo said, "If you work hard you will be respected, even if something goes wrong."

"Stand up to the situation and you will rise 10 feet tall," added Mario. "Colleagues will respect you for the example you set. Take responsibility and witness how peoples' respect for you grows."

Ravioli Rule: So you screwed up. Don't point the finger at others. That sets a bad example, especially if that's something you continually do. Take responsibility; otherwise, the up-and-coming Ravioli makers won't want to

---

work with you. We are at the stage of Ravioli making when we ought to know better.

Alfredo and Mario gave credit to Vittorio for a great job in making the Ravioli, preparing the meal and catering the entire DeBennedetto wedding. Vittorio was very happy. After the congratulations, Romeo approached Vittorio, an intense look in his eye. "You think you're hot stuff, don't you?" "I try to do the best I can," said Vittorio, trying not to be intimidated. "You think you are the best! But you're not!" He grasped Vittorio by the collar. "You think you are better than everyone else don't you? Well, I got news for you. I am better than you." He pushed him against the wall and walked away.

Vittorio was puzzled. He had helped Romeo in the past. He thought they were buddies. Why would personal accolades upset Romeo? After all, in the past, when Romeo received congratulations, Vittorio was always the first to offer him praise.

As a result of this incident, a positive personal relationship was permanently damaged. Vittorio was shocked by the jealously demonstrated. Nothing would ever be the same. A potentially positive collaboration was destroyed beyond repair.

Ravioli Rule: When colleagues receive credit for a great Ravioli-making event, celebrate the accomplishment. Their success is yours. It should be shared. Don't be jealous.

After a year of making pasta, Alfredo and Mario wanted to meet with people, collectively and individually, to pick their brains.

The meeting was set up with the full team and then broke off into units of smaller teams. All were charged with one responsibility: what can we do to make better Ravioli? The open-ended discussion involved everything from production to quality to style to types of Ravioli – as well as ingredients design, presentation and even catering. Each team was charged with coming up with ideas, and they did. The goal was to make better Ravioli.

"This approach can differentiate us from other Ravioli makers," declared Alfredo.

Mario nodded. He knew that he and his partner wanted to continually improve their Ravioli. "The 'Alfredo and Mario' Ravioli should be considered the best!" "Yes," exclaimed Alfredo, "ours should be the favored Ravioli."

One catering team, returning from a morning event, suffered a van breakdown. They had two flat tires and were stuck 40 miles from the Ravioli company. They realized they would not return in time to load up the deliverables for the next event, drive and prepare the table settings and food presentation. They called Alfredo and Mario and explained the timing and logistical situation. So Alfredo and Mario made a decision. They would cross-educate one of the Ravioli production teams, brief them on the catering team process and let them manage the loading of deliverables, table setting and start the food preparation and presentation.

This team worked in sync, preparing the tables and lining up the buffet dishes. They even became creative and suggested, for the future, to use elegant baroque style candle holders and placing the nametags of the food dishes in a golden frame. Alfredo and Mario were impressed. The fresh team provided an efficient operation and also demonstrated creativity. Earlier, Alfredo and Mario thought this would be a risky situation, but it turned out to be better than expected. There was value in using fresh people with other types of experience to offer new opportunities. From that day, Alfredo and Mario decided they would rotate people throughout the company. It provided everyone a new experience and an opportunity to offer ideas.

There was another purpose. All of them also became experienced in each area so they could be substituted at any time during high volume or absenteeism. If Alfredo and Mario needed to move resources around the company they could do so very easily and feel comfortable in the delivery of an efficient and quality product.

Ravioli Rule: After people have mastered how to make the Ravioli, move them to another Ravioli making area to share their experience. They can offer a fresh perspective and creativity with their new thinking. You can provide additional Ravioli experiences and a well-rounded education by rotating responsibilities among the team.

Once in a while, Alfredo and Mario would take turns and walk the Ravioli floor and go out with the teams during catering events. This was a good opportunity for Alfredo and Mario to keep their fingers on the pulse of the Ravioli managing/making process. They could see for themselves the quality of their thinking and work. They also recognized that some Ravioli makers may be intimidated with their efforts and success. As such, they tried to bring them in a more comfortable direction, a strategy designed to maximize their potential. Alfredo and Mario also found this as a good opportunity to motivate the people to keep them interested in the company, to look for future managers and to keep in touch with both the customer and the people working. In one instance, two of the new people were going to quit, but Alfredo and Mario encouraged them to stay, which later made them successful Ravioli managers.

Ravioli Rule: The head chef should make the Ravioli and talk with the Ravioli makers at anytime. It is good for the spirits and self-confidence of the team.

One of the new managers liked to have meetings with his team. He'd schedule meetings several times a day, sometimes to talk about nothing. He would schedule a meeting for 9AM, but he was always late. When he finally arrived, he would talk forever and get lost in minutia. He wanted to talk about the next steps in the Ravioli making process. His meetings went on and on, only because he got everyone's viewpoint and he did not make a decision – or he was afraid to make a decision. He summarized everyone's thoughts and did absolutely nothing. After the meeting, as people returned to their stations, their productivity was reduced because of the two hours lost. He decided to give them additional work and assign new Ravioli goals for the day.

This Ravioli management style was very frustrating and irritating. The team had the lowest productivity and morale. Most of the irritations stemmed from too many meetings with no clear purpose. Eventually, Alfredo and Mario, as they were having their one-on-one meetings with each team member and searching for the reason for low productivity, discovered the problem. The manager's meetings disrupted work flow. Alfredo and Mario made it a point to give this person feedback on meeting etiquette.

Ravioli Rule: Don't schedule meetings to talk about nothing. Maximize time.

One day, one of the new Ravioli makers asked one of the new managers a question during a team meeting, about the Ravioli making process. He wanted to know the difference between semolina flour and regular wheat flour and how it affected the process. Well, Antonio, the Ravioli manager, answered with such excruciating detail that it became boring and the point of the answer got lost. Antonio went on for 20 minutes and described the Ravioli making process from the beginning, through the history all the way to the presentation, and cleaning of the dishes. Alfredo and Mario, who attended this team meeting, later coached Antonio to answer questions specifically and concisely. This way you maximize the interest of the audience, maximize time and improve morale.

Ravioli Rule: Be prepared to concisely and clearly answer someone when asked a Ravioli-making question. Make the response simple and easy to understand. If they want more information about the Ravioli they will ask precise questions.

During one catering event everything was going wrong: the Ravioli were overcooked, the sauce was starting to burn, the tables were set with an odd number of settings instead of usual even numbers, the flowers arrived late and the bread was over-baked. The Ravioli manager got upset and yelled at all of the Ravioli makers.

This frustration started gradually. First, he exhibited frustration at each of them individually. He was so worked up he lined them all up in a room and yelled at everyone. The team was shattered and demoralized. They were expecting a pep talk to help them manage through this difficulty. Instead they were scolded. They were upset because they were yelled at right before the start of the event. They knew everything was going wrong; they didn't need to hear about it again during the catering event.

Ravioli Rule: Don't act in rage about the Ravioli going bad; learn to lead the Ravioli team to overcome the challenges.

Renato was a young Ravioli manager and he would always find time to have fun in the work environment. Sometimes he actually had too much fun. He wanted his people to be happy and felt that by making it fun all of the time, they too, would be happy, loyal and more efficient.

Before long he was having fun, party and games, rather than focusing on managing the efforts of the team. The team determined if he were a fun guy then he wouldn't mind if the team had more fun while he was out. This fun eventually had a profound impact, since the productivity level decreased, especially when the manager was away. If he wasn't serious enough to care about the Ravioli then he didn't care about them, either, and they shouldn't care about the Ravioli.

Ravioli Rule: *The Ravioli manager needs time for seriousness and time for play or celebration. This way the tone is set and the Ravioli makers know when to be serious, even when the Ravioli manager is away.*

Nunzio always came in about 45 minutes to an hour early to get his day started. He planned his day, had breakfast, got the day organized, spent time with his team and welcomed them. During this time, he occasionally met with Alfredo and Mario while they were getting their espresso. Others would arrive just in time as the day was starting. This was a big benefit for Nunzio, because it allowed him to rub shoulders with the top brass and with his team as well. It also allowed the top brass to see who was dedicated to making a commitment to the business. Nunzio eventually rose and became manager for district operations. Alfredo and Mario always saw this as a win-win situation, since either arriving early or staying late allowed you to bond with

all the Ravioli makers. It was good for the future leaders and it was good for Alfredo and Mario to spend time with the Ravioli makers.

Ravioli Rule: Get an early start and bond with the Ravioli makers. Those that don't meet and talk about the Ravioli will be out of the Ravioli.

The Frazano brothers would always arrive late just by a few minutes. Their Ravioli was always processed sloppily with little thought and always prone to error. When the Ravioli quality team was reviewing their Ravioli, they always appeared either overfilled, not perfectly cut or the edges were too close to the stuffing, which caused them to break apart when cooked. The Ravioli managers tried to demonstrate the importance of quality in the process. But to no avail; they still had the highest-level of quality rejects.

One day, the managers noticed the Frazano brothers' eyelids starting to close and their heads starting to bob. On another day, one manager saw them napping at lunchtime. So the assumption was they were tired and didn't get enough sleep. In one more week, Alfredo and Mario hit the jackpot. While they were heading into work, they passed the local bar and who was just walking out of the bar but the Frazano brothers. So they were tired, but not because they never got enough sleep, but because they were partying all night. Alfredo and Mario sat the boys down and explained very clearly the need for them to get a good night's sleep. They never came in late again and they never had any rejected Ravioli for lack of quality.

Ravioli Rule: As Ravioli makers, don't play too hard and don't try to eat the Ravioli from both ends. You need to get sufficient rest if you want to be efficient, effective and deliver quality.

Alfredo and Mario would walk the floor and a young Ravioli maker named Emilio would always talk to them and tell them how great they are and what a contribution they make to the Ravioli making process. Every day he would lavish incredible praise. Alfredo and Mario always smiled at the kind words. One day, when Alfredo and Mario were in the flour pantry looking over the quality and inventory of the semolina flour, they overheard Emilio come in, but he did not notice them in the pantry. He started complaining about Alfredo and Mario – that they didn't know what they were doing and how they stole their recipe from his relatives. The negative talk went on for five minutes. Alfredo and Mario walked past Emilio. He knew they heard him. Emilio never complimented them again on the floor.

Ravioli Rule: Sometimes people who continually sweet talk you aren't that sweet. Phony sweetness ruins the Ravioli.

The group decided to make gnocchi one day. They did a great job of making the new product with potatoes. It was simple. The potatoes were cooked in a pot of boiling water until done, peeled, let cooled and then mixed with eggs and flour to make these little delicious light guys of pasta.

One day, one of the efficiency people had an idea to make the process faster by peeling the potatoes first, then letting them cook in the boiling water until they were done and then mash them. It seemed beneficial because you didn't have to peel them while they were hot, or waste time by cooling them before peeling. Just move the peeling of the potato a step earlier will save time. Well, the problem, they found out, was that the peeled potato absorbs too much water and then it absorbs too much flour to compensate for the water. The gnocchi, instead of being light, became heavy and not very good. Losing the balance disturbs the gluten in the gnocchi and makes it heavy. This efficiency process, while first thought to save time, resulted in a poor and unacceptable quality pasta product. They returned to the old process.

Ravioli Rule: Sometimes the illusion of efficiency will negatively affect the quality of the product.

A catering event was held for the graduation of one of the neighborhood kids, little Enzo, at his home. Alfredo and Mario's catering team was responsible for setting up the event. It was a small affair, with immediate family for dinner and some other family and friends visiting for dessert.

So the team came over and started setting up the table, setting the dishes, utensils, the chaffing dishes, and the napkins. The food was delivered and warming up in the oven. The family was upstairs. But Enzo was sitting near the dinner table. The table was set and the candles were lit. While the team was in the kitchen, making final preparations, one of the candles started to drip wax on the tablecloth. Some of the warm dripping wax along with the buildup of wax was starting to slightly tip the candle. It could have been a disaster. Enzo was there watching. He looked at it and thought about what could happen. Just as he was reaching for the candle, it started to fall. One of the team members, Dom, walked in just in time to see Enzo grab the candle. Dom congratulated Enzo for taking action on something that could have been a catastrophe.

Enzo was not responsible and not the owner of the candle, since he didn't light it. However, he decided to become the owner, responsible for watching and taking action. He was an active Ravioli bystander. Dom thanked Enzo. If he didn't take action, the Ravioli catering event could have been disastrous.

Ravioli Rule: Take action on what you see is about to happen, even though you aren't in charge and aren't responsible. Take responsibility, ownership and do the right thing.

Alfredo and Mario were employing two people every day to shred the mozzarella cheese. It was time consuming. If the cheese was already shredded it would save them one day and two people, who could handle some other portion of the Ravioli making. So they went to their cheese supplier. Every month they diplomatically asked them to make shredded cheese. The suppliers said it was too much. They provide the mozzarella in bulk squares uncut or not at all. They had the market cornered. Not only were they the biggest suppliers, but no one else could match their business or their know-how. If they couldn't shred the cheese, certainly the smaller suppliers were not going to do it.

Alfredo and Mario kept talking to the manufacturer and actually found a way to make the mozzarella and shred it at the same time. They told the suppliers they could increase their cheese business by 25 percent with shredded mozzarella to sell to other restaurants and stores that needed shredded cheese. Alfredo and Mario discovered the need as they talked to different restaurants and found that there was an interest in shredded cheese. So the suppliers finally agreed and, indeed, their business did increase.

Ravioli Rule: If you build relationships and keep talking with your suppliers of cheese for the Ravioli they may eventually listen, understand the benefits of all sides and meet your needs.

One team member asked how the mozzarella cheese was made. So Alfredo and Mario were called in, since no one knew. Alfredo and Mario laughed and said, "There are some things you don't want to know how to make, such as sausage and mozzarella cheese."

Alfredo said that legend has it that mozzarella was first created when the milk curds accidentally fell into a big pasta pot of very hot water in a pasta factory in a small town in Italy. When the workers were picking up the curds, they stretched and then made mozzarella – and soon thereafter the first pizza was made. Of course, this was but one legend. There were many others. Indeed, every town in Italy has a story about how mozzarella was first created.

Basically, the principle involved in making all natural cheese is to thicken or curdle (or coagulate) the milk so it forms into curds and whey. Anyone who has left milk on the counter un-refrigerated for a period sees the milk curdle on its own. The milk sours and forms into an acid curd, and this is the start of making mozzarella.

Alfredo said, "After the coagulation sets the curd, the curd is then cut into bite size pieces."

Alfredo continued. "The next step is to heat the curds, or throw them into hot water—sometimes this is called shocking the mozzarella—and then they are stretched by hand and form strings. They are kneaded and stretched until smooth, then formed into round balls and placed in cold water to stop the cooking. This process makes fresh mozzarella cheese. It is time consuming, requires a lot of patience and work, but it is well worth the effort.

Ravioli Rule: Mozzarella cheese is made from something that looks bad. But after you shock it and give it time and patience, you can make excellent mozzarella.

One of the Ravioli teams really messed up and spoiled the Ravioli. The manager started yelling at the person he believed was responsible. "How could you do that? You should have more brains than that?"

Alfredo and Mario pulled the manager aside and encouraged him to find ways to discuss issues with his team rationally. Alfredo and Mario were hoping that he would follow their example.

The manager returned to the team and explained that he was just excited and passionate, he wanted them to succeed and he was hoping for a better result. He explained the reason for his high expectations. They understood him and then they worked harder the next day and weeks ahead. The positive environment resulted in a positive success.

Ravioli Rule: If the Ravioli did not cook right, don't scold the Ravioli maker as you would a child. Encourage the Ravioli maker to learn from the experience.

Alfredo and Mario were using their new machine for the round Ravioli. The machine came from northern Italy from a manufacturer only slightly known outside of the region of Northern Italy. The salesman offered to allow them to test the machine for one month with the hopes they would keep it.

When Alfredo and Mario made the Ravioli they found the texture of the dough was not as smooth as the homemade version they were making. One of the goals is to make smooth Ravioli dough that would taste velvety and soft. This machine changed that texture. They also tested this new Ravioli on some of the Ravioli makers and managers. All said that something was not right. They also blind tested the Ravioli in the café menus for lunch, with the same result. Alfredo and Mario decided they would not use the machine. It improved efficiency but not quality. "Our dough needs to be smooth. We are returning to basics," said Alfredo.

Ravioli Rule: Make sure that the new Ravioli making technology continues to retain the same quality as the machine making the original Ravioli. Make sure the machine is ready and reliable and contributes to the reputation of world class Ravioli.

One day, customers came into the Ravioli making store operation and looked at all the different Raviolis. There were pictures on the wall of all the different Ravioli and different parts of Italy, too. These people were getting excited about the variety. The store operations had refrigerators of Ravioli, manicotti, and stuffed shells. They were in awe.

This store allowed people to shop for all types of pasta. The window store fronts had plates filled with Ravioli and manicotti. They thought these were samples. So they picked them up, grabbed a fork and started to lift up the Ravioli. All of a sudden the whole Ravioli was stuck together. It was hard as a rock. They said, "These are not real Ravioli."

They realized these were samples that resembled Ravioli. They were a display product but looked very realistic – so realistic they looked authentic. There was even steam rising off the Ravioli, made by small tubes that emit steam to create an illusion of freshly baked Ravioli. The customers learned an important lesson: just because the Ravioli appear real doesn't mean they are real.

Ravioli Rule: Don't be fooled by the illusion. With experience you will know the difference and can recognize authentic Ravioli, and you should always make authentic Ravioli.

During a Ravioli making session, Alfredo and Mario decided to make this a little bit more exciting and had a contest: which team could make the Ravioli and the sauce with speed and accuracy. One team was on the money and made perfect Ravioli in record time.

The other team cracked under the pressure. Their Ravioli were soggy and the sauce burned. The winning team, since they achieved success so quickly in unison, harassed the other team. "We were faster and better. You certainly can't be better if you don't have the process down."

They tasted the competitor's Ravioli and spit it out. All this was done in full view of the other teams. Some laughed. Others ignored the harassment.

Mario and Alfredo walked in and saw this display and calmed the winning team down and then spoke with them. They advised the winning team to be gracious in winning and losing. You never know the losing team could possibly be the winning team next time and hopefully they will not humiliate you.

Ravioli Rule: Be gracious and professional to the Ravioli losers. Today's Ravioli losers could be tomorrow's Ravioli winners. Don't humiliate or embarrass today's Ravioli losers, they will be back and return the favor to you in their Ravioli victory.

As the company continued to grow, Alfredo and Mario realized they needed more space. So, they found a new building to house all these people and equipment.

In this new building, as they were getting settled into their location,

Mario was getting a ladder to stack the flour and semolina products in a two-story pile near each of the stations. He had to move them from the line of inventory to the individual teams' production center so they would be ready to mix the ingredients with eggs and water. As he was standing on his ladder high above the floor he noticed that there was a congregation of half of several teams near the water cooler. Another group of teams was talking near the Ravioli machines, out of view from Alfredo and Mario's office. Half of another group was standing near the machines, pretending to be working while the other half was sitting down out of view from Alfredo and Mario's office.

Watching this view from above, Mario realized what had been occurring and called Alfredo to get his opinion. Mario had a thought. After conferring with Alfredo, they decided that they would change their office to the second level and install a balcony catwalk around the working area to view the processing below.

Ravioli Rule: View Ravioli making from a higher level to get a new perspective and the full picture. You will see things you were unable to find before and a view of the whole operation in one picture.

The biggest event orchestrated by Alfredo and Mario was about to occur - a huge wedding with about 3,000 people. Alfredo and Mario realized that they did not have the capacity to make this Ravioli at one time. So they bought additional pots to boil the pasta. But they didn't have enough people or portable machines to make that much Ravioli. Make it in portions, they decided – a step at a time.

They prepared the Ravioli and the sauce in batches, stored them separately and created a short-term inventory. They managed the process by freezing the sauce and meatballs in advance and using it as necessary. On the wedding day, they timed the meal so that the Ravioli were made in batches by teams in various locations at the wedding. This way they presented the meal timely and this also provided many backups in case one location encountered a problem. The result: success.

Ravioli Rule: If time does not permit the full making of the pasta, think about making it in phases and spreading the Ravioli making process out over time.

Alfredo decided that he would have some people assist during the summer months while there were a high number of Ravioli makers on vacation. He visited the local high schools and colleges, offering opportunities for young people excited to learn about making Ravioli.

He hired about 30 over a 14-week period. Some worked the entire 14 weeks. Others worked eight weeks. Others were placed on a rotating basis based on the number of Ravioli makers on vacation. Mario taught them how to make Ravioli. First, they learned the theory and then they practiced. In the next step, they sat side by side with the people operating the Ravioli machines. By day five, they had to manage the process themselves.

After this process, they started making Ravioli the next week. The students were blended with different teams to assure maturity and professionalism; so all students weren't on the same team. This decision to separate the students would allow them to learn from seasoned Ravioli makers and to avoid clicking together and playing with people in their same age group.

One of the new boys came up with an idea to make different types of Ravioli – mini Ravioli, Ravioli rigati. He also starting thinking about valentine Ravioli made with tomato paste and shamrock Ravioli made with spinach for St. Patrick's Day. He was laughed at for his crazy ideas. Here was this young kid in high school thinking of different pastas. Veterans said, "Hey, this is the way we have made Ravioli. How could you come up with something so crazy?"

Alfredo and Mario held weekly sessions with these students to see how they were doing. So this young student asked a question about offering new Ravioli. Alfredo and Mario listened. When he finished his question, they thought about a new Ravioli product.

"Why not," said Mario.

"Let's try it," agreed Alfredo.

When Alfredo and Mario announced they were going to make shamrock Ravioli, team members couldn't believe what they were hearing. Alfredo and Mario praised this new person and gave him a week's vacation at their summer house as a reward. They said having new fresh people offers value because they look at what we have done with a fresh perspective.

"We provide them with experience and they provide us with opportunity and great suggestions," explained Mario. "We should allow such people to cultivate ideas. Starting today, anyone who has any ideas about new types of Ravioli should share."

Ravioli Rule: Don't stifle the creativity of a new person. If you don't allow new suggestions, the Ravioli will not remain fresh. Competitors will come up with new Ravioli, not you.

Alfredo and Mario were out at a theater watching the beautiful opera, "La Boheme." During intermission, they heard a stranger talk about Ravioli and pasta.

"It is unhealthy, the worst thing on your stomach," he said. Alfredo and Mario's ears perk up. Their hearts cried. Their favorite pasta, Ravioli, was being criticized. This person continued: "It is made with bad ingredients."

He wasn't talking about Alfredo and Mario's Ravioli, just Ravioli in general. He continued until it got to the point that Alfredo and Mario thought about interrupting, but they realized he did not know what he was talking about and that no one was listening to him. He was like an empty barrel making a lot of noise. His mind was closed. He could never accept the feedback from total strangers. They couldn't shock him, like hot water to make mozzarella. So, Alfredo and Mario walked back to their seats for the next scene.

On another day in town, a man in the center square talked about the downfall of the Ravioli and why it is bad for you. This man went on for half an hour telling stories—bad stories—about Ravioli. It is made with second-hand ingredients. The flour is from the bad farmlands of wheat that even bread companies would not buy. He asked, "Have you ever seen wheat fields in Italy? The water is not clean."

And he fabricated stories that did not make sense, like the Ravioli is not even homogenized. He had people believing him. That was the most frustrating thing for Alfredo and Mario. With this Alfredo and Mario decided they needed to rebut this misinformation. "I have a story for you about Ravioli," said Alfredo. "I don't know what he is talking about but let me share with you the facts."

"Let's hear the facts," said someone within the attentive crowd.

Alfredo and Mario related their story, and their family's story, and the generations of pasta makers. They started to explain how to make Ravioli at home and professionally. They provided details, like how the water is filtered twice for professionally made Ravioli. Listeners nodded their heads.

"If you like the quality of pasta from Italy then you should know that the flour is from the United States, from the great plains of South Dakota, from the finest wheat fields," explained Mario. "The flour is actually sent to Italy and ground for pasta, since there aren't enough wheat fields in Italy to supply the demand."

They made a persuasive argument. Alfredo added, "Ravioli is not supposed to be homogenized. That is for milk." The people cheered and started chanting, "Ravioli is good! Ravioli is good!"

The man came over to them afterwards and he said he felt bad about Ravioli because he had one bad experience. It was the night he ate Ravioli and then went to watch "La Boheme" and the pasta just lay in his stomach. He felt he was led astray and that he learned more about Ravioli today. He thanked them for the education.

Alfredo and Mario looked at each other and realized this was the guy from the theater that night. They felt good because their decision not to correct him was sound. He was too irritated that night. But defending the reputation of the Ravioli today was the right time and the right way.

Ravioli Rule: When it is the right time you need to speak up for the Ravioli and defend its honor, reputation and integrity.

Alfredo and Mario hired a veteran Ravioli maker from one competitor in another town. They believed his experience would be helpful. So, this man—Santini—joined the company and, because of his experience, he was made a middle manager of several teams. He turned out to be quite a Ravioli maker. He was so good that he was smarter than the Ravioli. He thought he knew everything. He wanted to change the flour to a lesser quality and change the amount of water and the eggs (medium size instead of large). He was smarter than the Ravioli – or so he thought. He was cocky, telling everybody how to do their job. He even talked to the Ravioli as if he knew best. He had no regard for the Ravioli. He thought he existed for the Ravioli; he was the gift to the Ravioli to make them perfect. This attitude did not sit well with Alfredo and Mario. Soon, Santini—called by his colleagues "Smartie

Santini"—was put out on the street.

The team learned a lesson: Never think you are smarter than the Ravioli.

Ravioli Rule: *Never, ever think you are smarter than the Ravioli.*

One of the new managers, Riggio, came from outside the company, and he was a quick learner. He had experience in the meatball making business, but he learned quickly about making Ravioli. He started managing different teams because of his experience. He helped one team get started, put the structure and processes together and then left someone else to manage.

When he connected with one of his new peers, Donato, he offered help. "If you need anything, I am here for you." Riggio was being a leader. But Donato was almost like Santini and said, "You did it your way. I am going to do it my way."

Riggio was taken aback. But he simply smiled, walked away and scratched his head. Subsequently, it didn't take long for this new manager, Donato, to start screwing things up. He didn't know which end was up and started becoming overwhelmed. He never went to Riggio for advice. Riggio was helping another team and was unaware of the problem.

Riggio often thought of his offering of assistance and just couldn't believe that this new manager could not listen and resisted help. All he had to do was say "thank you," smile and Riggio never would have thought anything of it. But instead he was a brash, obnoxious, a know-it-all. The experience had annoyed Riggio so much that he made sure the people on his team learned to do the right thing. They should always thank someone who offered assistance, take them up on the offer and learn from the experience. The person who offered will be flattered and will always remember you in a positive way.

Ravioli Rule: *Whenever anyone offers advice and counsel, never say no. You may learn something if you say yes, I look forward to talking with you.*

A quiet and dedicated young person from Italy who worked as a part-time Ravioli maker with Alfredo and Mario while going to school, recently finished his education in finance and accounting. Alfredo and Mario decided to hire him back, but this time as an assistant manager in the accounting business area. He worked balancing the books, creating ledger sheets and managing inventory.

After the first month's balance sheets were completed, he strolled on the floor and worked with some of his old teammates and watched them as they worked the Ravioli and he smiled as he watched the efficiency and teamwork. He watched them as they maneuvered with a new machine that created fettuccine with ridges, the first of its kind. He watched as the machines started making new types of pasta, papardelle, and linguine. He liked this so much that he started working in the Ravioli shop, once a month, for an entire day. He shared stories with the Ravioli makers, remembering his roots and thanking them for maintaining their quality and management.

Alfredo and Mario thought working with the Ravioli production teams was a good idea and decided that all their non-Ravioli making managers should participate in the production. It was a good way to remind everyone how critical the Ravioli maker's job was and make the teams feel important.

Ravioli Rule: As a Ravioli manager, if you worked the Ravioli floor, remember your roots and recognize the changes in the process, keep your relationships with the Ravioli makers and the process so it will keep you fresh and up to date with the changes. By maintaining these relationships you also provide an inspiration to the team. They know you are authentic.

Another Ravioli maker was promoted to foreman and did a great job. But as a manager, he was more interested in showing off and impressing the upper managers and not managing his team. He became interested only when management walked around his area. He looked good, wore his cooking attire, including the chef hat, had his shoes polished. He placed some flour on his pants, hands, hair and face and appeared to be working but he moved out in time to say hello to the upper managers.

When the people asked what is important today he said, "Impressing management." He worked his team by providing miscommunication, that impressing the managers is the priority. When something went wrong, no matter how small, he yelled at them. He never complimented them and never told them that they did a good job. He wanted them to do better to impress the managers and did not care about the substance of the daily routines of making Ravioli. His priority was to replace the variable of doing What is Important Now with the variable of Who do I Impress Now. He made sure he was actively visible when senior managers were around.

He had the team waste time by cleaning machines at the completion of the Ravioli making cycle, not at the end of each day. This reduced efficiency and production. He had the Ravioli makers spend time with him in meetings, saying a lot and doing little, as senior managers walked by. Eventually the senior managers figured out what was going on, based on production quotas and employee complaints.

Alfredo and Mario had a talk with all managers and the team. They explained the importance that What's Important Now always equals Who do I Impress Now. That is the real WIN = WIN situation. When you manage What is Important Now it will be equal to Who do I Impress Now. Once the calculation is thrown off you lose, because you lose sight of the Ravioli making purpose and values. When the priority is placed on Who Do I Impress Now, it cancels out the equation.

Ravioli Rule: When you focus on impressing others, you will lose sight of how to make the Ravioli.

This time they hired some additional people to the Ravioli making process. There was one Ravioli manager and one Ravioli maker on two different teams that really stood out. It was amazing what they could do, not what they accomplished, but what they could do to make a team so dysfunctional.

The Ravioli manager did nothing but talk about himself. He was focused on self-centered behavior. No other person was important as him. No other person could tell such great stories. This person became unbearable. He considered himself a gift to the company. He would say, "I look good dressed in black."

If he was going on an expensive trip, he would talk about it the whole week with no regard for people who could not afford that kind of vacation. He became a disruptive presence. People felt he liked to rub his success in their faces. The Ravioli manager was condescending and treated everyone as subordinates. He did nothing but watch them work. When there was a mistake or even the slightest perception of a mistake he would ridicule people forever and he never forgot it, even if they learned from the mistake. This manager would question them forever as if they were on a witness stand. He would delegate work goals to them late in the afternoon and expect it to be done first thing in the morning.

The other new person, the new Ravioli maker did not understand his role. He would treat his colleagues as if they worked for him, and he demanded they respond quicker and faster to make up for his lost time. He would demand they respond to his requests immediately and always complained when there was a negative answer to his request. The Ravioli makers started to resent him, because if he did not get an answer immediately he would find someone else who could and then he would verbally throw them into the Ravioli machine and bad mouth them for his aggravation. He almost assumed he played the role of manager, but arrogantly. This Ravioli maker thought he was Alfredo and Mario, but only not nice.

Both of the teams started to provide feedback to Mario and Alfredo, who decided to have individual meetings with the team members to receive more personal feedback. Mario and Alfredo let both of these people leave quietly.

Ravioli Rule: *It is amazing how one Ravioli person can disrupt and mess up the process, generate disorder and chaos, when it takes so many people working as a team, so hard to make it right.*

Alfredo and Mario enjoyed the fruits of their labor. The company continued to grow. Alfredo and Mario were still involved in making decisions

and micro-managing even little decisions, like the amount of boxes to be ordered to hold their Ravioli in the refrigerator, or about the type of food to order for the teams that were working late on special catering events. Should they have pizza, Chinese food, fast food? Sometimes Alfredo and Mario were called at home to make the decision. This continued for about a year. It frustrated the 500 Ravioli makers so much they started to make jokes about Alfredo and Mario not allowing anyone to make simple decisions (like should we have two-ply toilet paper or one-ply paper, should the floors be mopped and waxed once a month or just mopped and then waxed every six weeks?)

The managers decided to approach Alfredo and Mario to let them free up some of the day-to-day simple decisions for the managers to handle and let Alfredo and Mario manage the short- and long-term strategic decisions.

Alfredo and Mario were unaware of the consequence of their decisions. They thought they were being asked for input and had no idea the impact this was having on people. They made the immediate decision that day-to-day decisions were to be made by the managers and that even the Ravioli makers could be empowered to make certain decisions.

Alfredo and Mario thanked the managers for coming forward. "We don't want to stifle the thought process, we want people to be mature," said Mario. "We want to respect them and treat them like adults, not like some toddlers unable to make decisions. Alfredo agreed: "We are not caretakers for children, we are managers of people and they are capable of making decisions."

Ravioli Rule: *If you are the only Ravioli manager making all the decisions, especially on minute details, you need to learn how to empower others to make the decisions. Otherwise, you are high level babysitters*

Alfredo and Mario decided they should have some of their better managers start selling their products—the Ravioli, sauces and just plain catering events—to customers. They decided to sell at restaurants, schools, and churches. They looked for catering opportunities by reviewing the newspapers for graduations, births, and engagements. This became very successful, and Alfredo and Mario had several people working on and selling these opportunities.

One month, one of the members, Donni, did not reach his goal and was getting disappointed and depressed. His team members were having a successful month. So one of the team members, Miguel, said, "Don't worry, it will work out. You have other opportunities you are working on that will solidify next month or the following month. This is just a dry selling time for you. You will make it up in the future."

Donni felt relieved and thanked him for his support.

The following month the situation was reversed, Donni had twice the sales he normally does. Miguel was right, but this time Miguel was in a dry selling time.

Donni kept asking Miguel, "How many sales do you have this month?"

Miguel responded, "Very few." "Well, I got mine," Donni said. "I got twice the ones I had last month. Too bad you don't have any. I am the greatest salesman that Alfredo and Mario have."

This disturbed Miguel especially since he organized the team members to support Donni as a team player during his dry sales month. Miguel and the rest of the team decided that Donni was not a team player. He is just here for himself and they would no longer support him or provide guidance to him in the future.

Ravioli Rule: Remember to thank a manager who during your tough times provided you with counsel and sound advice. Be sure to return the support when the situation is reversed.

Alfredo and Mario paid a lot of attention to Ravioli managers and makers. Every day, and for almost half the day, they were on the production floor holding team meetings, talking to all the managers and makers. It was a good relationship, with synergy. Alfredo and Mario believed if you made them feel good, they would feel good about making the Ravioli.

Well, the people that managed the receiving and distribution of the flour and eggs to make the pasta felt disenfranchised. Alfredo and Mario never visited them or had a floor meeting. They started calling themselves the stepchildren or distant relatives. The Ravioli team was considered the favored child.

One of the workers made his frustrations known. He felt the area he represented was not recognized as an integral part of the Ravioli making process. He felt this way because they were far from the process and because

Alfredo and Mario did not visit them often, only when they walked to or from their cars, saying good morning or goodnight.

Alfred and Mario decided to act on it. They started visiting the area every day, held team meetings, and had them rotate into the Ravioli production shop and also had the Ravioli makers take turns in the receivable and delivery area. Alfred and Mario also made an analogy – that without the receiving and delivery team, we would not get our jobs started because "they maintain the inventory of flour and eggs. They organize the receipt of the raw materials and deliver them early in the morning before the teams arrive, so the Ravioli makers could get their job started without any holdups. The receiving and delivery team was integral to the start of the morning."

Alfredo and Mario called them "the keys to start the Ravioli engine."

This process recognizes everyone as important, and it also passes additional skills onto the other people. It also represents a potential back up team in case people were absent.

As a result, the people from the receiving and delivery area were happier and felt like they belonged to the team and felt closer to the organization, because they knew Alfredo and Mario and knew them well.

Ravioli Rule: Treat all people with respect and with a high regard for their job, even if it is not a direct role in the production operations. As Ravioli managers you should demonstrate how each job contributes and is a valuable part of the delivery of the Ravioli making process.

One day one of the senior managers, who never came to see the process work, heard that one of the Ravioli was not made on time and not the right size. As a result, this manager, who was locked in a Ravioli tower and oblivious to the process, came down and made the overcorrection. He believed that the entire process was flawed and asked that the people and managers track all the Ravioli made and measure them by size and count the time it took to make the Ravioli. If a Ravioli maker was off by 10 seconds or the Ravioli was the wrong size, they went on the Ravioli exception report and were reported to senior managers.

This overcorrection caused a lot of agita (heartburn and upset stomach) among the makers and managers. Almost a whole new person was needed to come in and take responsibility for measuring the entire time and size of the Ravioli. It slowed down the process and made everyone feel incompetent.

It took about four months until senior managers had faith in the team again, and at that point they removed the tracking of the Ravioli by time and size.

Ravioli Rule: Don't make overcorrections for one wrongly made Ravioli. Overcorrection stifles work, destroys confidence and morale. Find the right correction. You also need to get down from the Ravioli tower and visit the production team.

In the early days, when Alfredo and Mario were younger and just starting to cater events, their team wasn't always precise and on the Ravioli. Now the team is prepared, practical and seasoned. They are veterans. Today, the business is well organized, disciplined, well structured, and the timing is impeccable. They told this story:

For one catering event they had 20 people to help them out and sometimes it seemed like they were 20 six-year-olds. They splintered off into groups, disorganized with no focus. Some of them made the Ravioli before the sauce was ready, the Ravioli were already cooked and about to be served in plates that weren't placed on the tables. The sauce wasn't even cooking and the Ravioli were ready. The guests were not arriving for two more hours. The team was not well briefed on the process and event time frame. There was a lack of communication between managers and the team.

Alfredo and Mario arrived to see the progress the team was making and took charge of the project and managed to prioritize and organize the event to maximize the resources and deliver a wonderful presentation. By the time the guests arrived, everything ran very well and the guests were unaware of any mishaps.

The next day Alfredo and Mario educated all the managers and the teams on the right process and procedures for managing and catering an event. They said the goals and the timetable needed to be clear and understood from the start. This way, everyone knows their roles and learns the roles of others.

Ravioli Rule: As managers, make sure all the makers know the goals, objectives and timetable for the presentation.

The team was preparing for the second biggest event of the year, a large catering banquet. One week before the event, Mario hurt his back and was unable to attend to business. Alfredo was traveling, searching for a new supplier of wheat. Well, Mario called Raquel, one of the managers, and asked her to manage the catering event. Every day Mario would call and ask for the update and provide succinct advice to Raquel. Mario would keep his calls concise, managing Raquel's time efficiently.

The big day came and everything worked perfectly. This was a Ravioli making team of 20 who had their act together. All aspects of the production and delivery worked flawlessly – from the setting of the tables, the placing of the linens and plates, candles; even the table linen was secured to avoid being blown by the wind. The team thought of everything.

The Ravioli were well made, the sauces were checked to ensure they remained hot and not burned, all Ravioli items were checked to maintain freshness, drinks were served with a smile and guest were treated royally. Team attitude was positive – representing a true ownership of the people who believed that each was responsible for their task and responsible as a team.

After the event, Raquel had a quick meeting and thanked everyone for both their individual and team efforts and told them that each of them were responsible for a successful catering event: "All of you, kept up your attitude and work ethic, had a great role in making the best Ravioli and will enjoy continued success at our company."

When Mario returned to work he thanked Raquel for her efforts. The family that had the event called Mario and thanked him for catering such a beautiful party. The family almost chose someone else—a better and well-known pasta caterer—but family members were glad they choose the lesser known Alfredo and Mario. They were going to have Alfredo and Mario again as a caterer and spread the word about the outstanding job his team performed. Mario thanked the customer and sent over a special complimentary tray of Ravioli.

Mario thanked Raquel for her success. Mario then thanked the team in charge of the event and provided everyone with a special note of appreciation, in front of all the other teams. Mario decided that he would have a special dessert for this team and let all the other teams share in the recognition. He believed that by including the other teams, he would foster support and continued success. He publicly thanked Raquel for a superb job and said that Raquel could substitute for him at any time and that all of them had a great opportunity to become great Ravioli managers. Raquel's colleagues also thanked her for a great job and making all of them look good.

Ravioli Rule: *Letting Ravioli makers share in the joy and achievement of a successful event will encourage everyone to make great Ravioli events, too.*

Alfredo and Mario have now been in the business for 10 years and there is a Ravioli manager that has been working for them for a little over nine years. He started as a trainee, then a Ravioli maker and then manager. Every day he came in and worked as hard as he did the first day. He had the same affect on his team, which on average stayed longer and had a better attitude than some of the other teams. Mario and Alfredo asked him how he maintained his enthusiasm.

"It's easy," he said. "I just think of two things. One is that I come to work as if it was my first day and, second, I am only as good as my next Ravioli."

Ravioli Rule: *Every time you make the Ravioli, think of it as your first day and that you are only as good as your next Ravioli.*

Alfredo and Mario were asked many times for their opinions about their favorite pasta or their favorite sauce. Some people would believe that whatever pasta they saw them eat was their favorite.

One Friday night Alfredo and Mario were out to dinner and close to them was a table of some of the Ravioli makers—who were hidden from view—and they heard Alfredo and Mario say their favorite pasta was tortellini. This comment was taken out of context, and by mid-Monday, the story had changed to several variations. One variation was they didn't like the Ravioli and the people that made them. They were going to change the company to tortellini makers instead of Ravioli makers. Another story was that they were selling the business to a tortellini company.

Well, Alfredo and Mario heard about rumors and decided to have a team meeting to put an end to this story. They clarified they are Ravioli makers first, that someone may have heard about their love of pasta and this weekend they said to each other that tortellini is one of their favorite – only second to the best one which is the Ravioli.

Ravioli Rule: *Sometimes comments, public or private, have unknown and far reaching impact and may impress and impact others negatively or positively. When you hear them, and if they are incorrect you need to set the story straight.*

One day the Ravioli managers were impressed with this new Ravioli maker, Pia. She got the job done. Every time the manager asked for something, she took care of it. And she made the Ravioli perfectly. Her job area was clean and it was always cleaned before anyone else's.

But it didn't take long to see that she wasn't all she pretended to be. Alfredo and Mario watching on the balcony catwalk, saw her pick up all the teams' objects and stuff them in a closet. She never cleaned properly. She took shortcuts in cleaning the machines. They weren't properly sterilized and ready for the next day. She only worked on what was important and visible to the manager. Other critical Ravioli components were left unattended, such as having the right inventory. When inventory was low, she went over and smiled to a member from a different team and asked for additional flour or eggs. She never went to the same person twice. It was eventually catching up with her. She ended up dropping the ball on a number of production deliverables. The short story is that she was soon relieved of her responsibilities.

Ravioli Rule: Making Ravioli the right way is more than just doing the visible; it is doing the invisible, because eventually the invisible will become visible.

One day when Alfredo and Mario were at a relative's house for a family party, the family decided to make Ravioli, of course. This Ravioli was a bit different – large and round with fluted edges. Instead of ricotta inside, they were filled with a mixture of portabella mushrooms pureed with mortadella, prosciutto and finally ricotta cheese. The sauce was different, too. It was made with oil, walnut, breadcrumbs, anchovies and cheese.

So, the Ravioli were presented and the maker, manager and owner of the Ravioli decided to taunt Alfredo and Mario. He presented and served Ravioli to all the guests, except to Alfredo and Mario. He said, "So you think you're big shots. Well, you haven't tried mine. You want mine, go ahead and get it. You want it, it's all yours, but I am not serving it to you. You know what? You think you make the best Ravioli. Well, mine are so good, you don't even have to eat them."

At first, it sounded like fun and people were laughing, but it deteriorated and became obnoxious. People were turned off when they heard him say to Alfredo and Mario, "You know what, don't do me a favor, don't try them. You know why, because I never tried yours."

It got so bad that some of the guests put their plates down and stopped eating. Alfredo and Mario left. The obnoxious maker said, "Good, you want to go, go ahead but remember I offered you my Ravioli, the best in town and you left it all and walked away. You know what, you can't make my Ravioli."

With that, the people started to clear out and now he was by himself eating his Ravioli, all alone.

Ravioli Rule: Don't get obnoxious when you think you hold all the Ravioli.

Now, Alfredo and Mario told the story about when they were younger their parents took them on a trip to their hometown in Italy to show their boys how the Ravioli were made old-world style. So off they went to travel to the country they called the home of the Ravioli. Mom and dad remembered how their own parents said the townspeople made Ravioli in the streets from pots filled with water and packages of flour lining the street. When you walked into town, the people were making Ravioli on the street, enjoying each other's company.

So, they took the trip to Italy and when they all arrived there were no pots, no flour. Nobody was making Ravioli. There were people selling sausage and peppers in special pizza bread and warm chestnuts in a paper cone.

"Where are the Ravioli makers?" "They are at home making the Ravioli," a man told them. "Why do you think they should be out here on the street?" "Well yes, that is where they were before, when we were little in this town with our parents," dad observed.

The man laughed and said, "That was how we made things before, when no one had a kitchen in their home and all people pooled their resources to make the Ravioli. That has changed, we have evolved. You missed the evolution, we are modern now. We make Ravioli in our home."

Ravioli Rule: You think the Ravioli making process is frozen in time. You were not there to watch the evolution and change in process. You need to remember that the Ravioli making process may change.

Alfredo and Mario decided they should offer a culinary experience to people who either wanted to experience the Ravioli or the people who wanted to learn how to make it. So they decided to offer an event at their restaurant, called "A Tour of Italy." They advertised this for one month. They had prepared a wide variety of Italian pastas with different sauces from regions of Italy. They emphasized the different type of pasta and cooking styles with each area of Italy. The event was well planned and organized.

They had 500 people attend this event, a variety. Some came to learn how the Ravioli were made and were very interactive with the chefs. They asked very pointed and detailed questions. Alfredo and Mario even had teachers who were from the different areas of Italy and who offered tips on the different types of wine in the region, the culture of the region, including the variation on language as well as the styles of cooking.

Alfredo and Mario walked around and spoke with most of the people, who were very intrigued about the pasta and spent time with the teachers learning about the culture. Some of the people attending were dressed as if they were going to a wedding. Alfredo and Mario watched these people and noticed that they didn't eat the Ravioli, didn't go to the teachers to learn about the culture and they never went to the Ravioli making kitchen counters to watch the nine different masters make their Ravioli. Alfredo and Mario realized these people were just here to be part of the crowd. They were Ravioli groupies, to show people they were with the "in crowd," to look good and not learn the substance of understanding how to make the Ravioli. They never even ate the Ravioli. They were here for themselves. They missed the opportunity to try a new experience – the Ravioli.

Ravioli Rule: Some people want the Ravioli for the wrong reason, because they exist for themselves and want to impress people. They are not there to enjoy the culinary experience from beginning to end and miss the learning and sharing.

Alfredo and Mario told this story about being prepared. When they were younger, their mom always made extra sauce and meatballs and sausage. The boys asked, "Why did she make so much?

"You never know when you need it," she said. "What do you mean," they asked. "Well, it is good because we can have leftovers for the week," she replied. "But it is also good when we have some people unexpectedly over for dinner. We are always prepared."

So one Sunday, a few weeks later, some of cousins stopped by with some pastries in the early afternoon. The conversation extended for a while and they stayed for dinner. Dinner was effortless. All mom had to do was add more pasta since there was enough sauce, meatballs and sausage for everyone. The event turned out fine.

Two weeks later, the boys had five friends over. Mom asked them to stay for dinner. One friend said to Alfredo, "No, thank you. It would be too much work for your mom."

"Don't worry, we have enough food for everyone," Alfredo assured. "Yeah," said Mario. "Mom always says all we have to do is just put on another pot of pasta."

Alfredo added, "If she had been in Boston during the revolutionary war and Paul Revere was running through the streets saying 'the British are coming,' Mom would say, 'It's okay, we will put on another pot of pasta'."

Ravioli Rule: *It is good to have extra Ravioli and sauce so you are prepared for any surprise events.*

Another manager thought the more Ravioli you gave the team to make, the more the team developed – his reasoning was that they produced and the team became better because they learned to deliver more Ravioli.

One manager, Carmine, decided he was going to throw everything at the team. So he had them making the biggest vat of Ravioli ever. Then, as they were making this Ravioli he came in and asked the team to make spinach Ravioli. Then one hour later as they were working on this project he told them to make Ravioli nudi, which are the stuffing without the pasta covers. He kept giving them different pasta to make over a two-week period that they got exhausted and went to talk to Alfredo and Mario. When they heard this story, they decided they would talk to Carmine about the famous Myth of Sisyphus and how Carmine's actions multiplied the myth into larger proportions and demoralized the team.

The Myth of Sisyphus is about frustration – about a man rolling a large rock up a hill. The goal is to get the rock to the top of the hill, but as soon as the rock almost reaches the top it rolls back down the hill and he has to start over.

In this case, the myth was overwhelming because Carmine not only made the rock larger, he kept throwing other large boulders down the mountain and expected the team to manage it all. Not only were there new boulders but Carmine also increased the size of the hill to a mountain each time they got another project.

Ravioli Rule: As a Ravioli manager, know when you are putting the makers in a Sisyphus environment. You will lose the effectiveness of the team if you make the hill into a mountain and add more work. You need to know how to balance the effort and workload.

One person who ate the Ravioli at one of the catering events complained and complained – first to the family who held the event and then to one of the catering managers. The family approached Alfredo and Mario and said that some people were complaining about the food, the meatballs were hard and the Ravioli were overcooked.

Alfredo said, "We have a quality taste test to make sure the Ravioli is al dente and the meatballs are tender." "Some people say the food is not good," he was told. So Alfredo and Mario asked the hosts if they tried the food and if they were pleased with it.

"Why, yes, we thought it was good until this person said that they were not done right." "Have any other guests complained" asked Alfredo. "No.

Only this person, Pompei." "Who is he?" asked Mario.

"Pompei, I forget his last name," said the host. "Why don't you bring Pompei here and we will get some clarity and hopefully some answers."

So Pompei came to the meeting and they asked him, "Why do you think our Ravioli were bad?" He said. "They just tasted bad." When they pursued additional questioning, he just said everything was bad, with no further explanation, and that he told the other guests.

After a few minutes of questioning they realized this person was just an irritant and wanted to create problems. Alfredo and Mario researched it and handled it correctly and concluded that this person should not be believed. So off they went and the hosts were fine too.

Ravioli Rule: Don't take criticism about the Ravioli at face value, because it may not always be correct. Always research and probe until you verify and have clarity in the criticism.

One day Alfredo and Mario were having individual conversations with different Ravioli managers about the details of processing the dough and the machines that were used. Each manager had a different process or view about the Ravioli-making machine and there was neither uniformity nor an understanding of the machines. So Alfredo and Mario decided to have another meeting with the managers to discuss the correct process for the Ravioli and make sure all had the same understanding and that there was consistency.

As each individual talked, they learned from one another, but also with Alfredo and Mario's assistance, they also recognized that not all of them had accurate information. Alfredo and Mario did a brilliant job of making each of them understand that they did not have the complete picture. The team understood; they made conclusions based on incorrect perceptions. They gained experience at gathering the right information and finally realized that all of them are smarter than just one of them.

Ravioli Rule: Use the full 360-degree round Ravioli approach to make a good decision. Get all Ravioli managers/makers in the same room and you will get different opinions, approaches and accurate/inaccurate information on the same process. Everyone will also hear each other's perspective, perceptions and learn to get the right information to make the right decision.

Alfredo and Mario hired two cousins, Pablo and Paulo, who had experience in making Ravioli. They were hired as Ravioli managers and were located on two different floors. After two months the production levels with both teams were about equal, with Paulo just slightly ahead of Pablo. They also had two different ways of managing people, which affected performance.

Paulo's team was just slightly ahead of Pablo's team, but there was a marked difference in the teams' dispositions. Pablo's team was miserable. When they arrived at work their body language was horrible. They walked with their heads down. They would avoid eye contact, they never smiled, and they never talked to anyone.

On the other hand, Paulo's team was happy. They laughed as a team, they walked proudly and all of them interacted well. You could see the difference as the two teams work. Pablo's team was serious. No interaction. Their faces reflected misery and unhappiness. When Pablo walked away from the team, members started whispering and sneering. Paulo's team was happy and smiling with each other when they worked.

Alfredo and Mario decided to have conversations with the team members when their managers were away. They learned that Paulo's team was happy because of his management style. Paulo welcomed each of them in the morning. He did work them hard but he had their best interests at heart. Paulo worked on their career development, instilled pride in each of them and made them feel more confident and more comfortable in their responsibilities. They always knew that Paulo was looking out for their best interests.

In contrast, Pablo's team was miserable because their manager treated them badly. In fact the team was using the "b" in Pablo as an initial for bad manager. He treated them with little respect, like they were four year olds. He would yell at them, told them everything they did was wrong and never recognized their hard work. One time, during a successful Ravioli-making event, he even said it was about time they worked hard. He was long on criticism, short on gratitude.

The team recalled an incident. Pablo complained when anyone left work on time so they could get their dry cleaning before the store closed. He even reprimanded one individual about this. He thought he should stay later and find a new dry cleaner with extended hours. Pablo, though—setting a bad managerial example—would take time off in the afternoon to get a haircut or take his car in for an oil change. This hypocritical behavior irritated the team.

They worked hard because they were afraid of the manager, not because they respected him. Conversely, Paulo's team worked hard because they had hope for their future, knew that their manager had their best interests at heart, inspired them and they respected their manager.

Ravioli Rule: Smart Ravioli managers are sincere and authentic and have the best interest of their team at heart. They build relationships with the team and treat members with respect. Because of this, the Ravioli makers assume responsibility/ownership for their Ravioli making.

During a Ravioli dinner, Alfredo and Mario watched Uncle Zio, who is eating their Ravioli for the first time. He said not a word during the dinner. While everyone else was enjoying their dinner and laughing, Uncle Zio just sat there with his arms folded. He then took a bite of the Ravioli, laid his fork down. He waited to swallow, picked up his fork again and ate the rest of the Ravioli. He still didn't talk. His face was expressionless. When the dishes were picked up and the table cleared everyone looked at him waiting to hear his disapproval.

"Well?" asked Alfredo and Mario. Uncle Zio responded, "I don't want to offend any family here today, especially my wife, but these are very good Ravioli, boys, very good!" Alfredo and Mario were surprised and they learned that sometimes a person's body language is not really a reflection of their actual thoughts and feelings.

Ravioli Rule: Understand and learn that body language is not always a good measurement. Take time to reflect on the body language that you give off, as well.

One of the customers said, "This is the third time this year that I have had you cater my events. Maybe you should reward me with the fourth event and give me a few pounds of Ravioli for free."

Alfredo and Mario thought about this and realized that the idea represented a good opportunity to build loyalty and relationships with customers. So, they offered customers three free pounds of Ravioli with every fourth catering event. The sales tactic proved a big hit. Later they added six pounds after eight catered events.

Ravioli Rule: *Create an opportunity for your customers to return. Innovate ways to continue the relationship and maintain loyalty.*

One day, one of the customers said that they wanted to have a large reunion for 10,000 people with more than 75,000 Ravioli to be made within the next four days. Alfredo and Mario realized they could not make this amount in such a short time and informed the customer of the decision. They learned it was okay to say no, and they learned when you had to say no.

Ravioli Rule: *Learn when you have to decide to turn down a Ravioli-making project.*

Conclusion - Ravioli Rules

Time has passed. Alfredo and Mario shared their story with their grand-daughters, who are now much older. The story, was related over many years. Abigail and Theresa have finished college and have put their learning to good use. Alfredo and Mario are now in their 80s. In the lifelong conversations with their grandparents, the girls realized there were themes of these lifetime experiences and they have developed the themes under - what else –RAVIOLI.

"Gramps," the girls said, "we have a great 'thank you' for you. You taught us the Ravioli Rules. We want to thank you by sharing the themes we learned from you, so we can continue to use our Ravioli experiences!"

Both grandfathers said simultaneously, "What is it girls?" They both said, "Well, let me tell you the good news, the themes are all based on the word Ravioli! They are the Ravioli Rules!"

The grandfathers said, "What do you mean?" All four were laughing because they all realized that they were all asking and answering at the same time.

"Well, let me show you. Let's start with the letter R."

R

RIGHT

R is for making Ravioli the Right Way. This is the basic ingredient and starting point for all the Ravioli Rules. The Right way is guided by the Ravioli Rules. It is about making the Right decisions and choices for the Ravioli maker and for the customer. This is very simple, it is cooking with common sense, but sometimes, common sense is uncommon for some and as a result they don't make Ravioli the Right way.

Doing things the Right way is easy for some Ravioli makers/managers because they follow the Ravioli Rules; it is part of their Values to do the Right thing and make things Right. It is based on exercising sound judgment. Great Ravioli makers/managers continue to exercise good judgment after they learned it from experience. Great Ravioli are always made, by great Ravioli managers/makers making Ravioli the Right Way. The Right way always wins!!

RESPECT

It is crucial for Ravioli managers and makers to Respect the Ravioli. Respecting the Ravioli takes various forms. It is learning to have Respect for the Ravioli making process, the Ravioli makers/managers, the Ravioli customer and finally the Ravioli itself. Respect is consideration and holding the Ravioli in high regard. Respect leads to open and fair communication. Respect provides feedback instead of criticism. You have faith and trust in each other for success in making the Ravioli. Respect allows you to understand all the Ravioli managers/makers viewpoints, opinions and suggestions. Finally, Respect leads to increased morale, harmony and better Ravioli.

READY AND RELIABLE

Ready and Reliable Ravioli managers/makers need to be Ready to get the job done. They need to be prepared, trained, educated, and mentally Ready for the job. They need to be Ready for immediate requests for Ravioli making tasks or changing responsibilities at a moment's notice. In its simplest form, Ready means you show up to work on time, don't leave work early, don't play at work and do your best to get the job done. It is the Ravioli Work Ethic.

Reliable means that you are dependable. You can be counted on to get the Ravioli made – to get the job done with little direction. When you are given a task to complete the Ravioli, it is done. If there are obstacles, you find ways around them. You can be trusted when you are consistently Reliable and people know the Ravioli will be made when you say they will be made. Consistent Reliability may lead to additional responsibility. In addition to people being Ready and Reliable, the pasta machines need to be Ready and Reliable to make the Ravioli, too!!

RISKS

Ravioli managers take and manage many Risks. There are many, from start up Risks, people Risks and process Risks. However, if the Ravioli is good or bad, if the Ravioli customers are happy or unhappy, it affects the most important risk, which is the Reputation Risk. This Relationship Risk is the hardest one to control and overcome if the Reputation is ruined. Great Ravioli managers/makers are comfortable to develop strong relationships while managing Reputation Risk. Reputation Risk taking is rewarding because it allows for improvement, change, results in success and great Ravioli.

REFLECTION

Reflection is necessary for self-assessment, which leads to learning and personal growth. It is in Reflection that you assess your achievements, strengths, weaknesses and opportunities. It is a thoughtful process that will lead to improved Ravioli. Reflection is a time of thinking and reviewing current situations to develop creative solutions, or enter a new phase of improvements.

RESILIENCE AND RECOVERY, NOT RESIGNATION

Resilience and Recovery, not Resignation is used at times when it seems all the Ravioli are falling apart, but you need an inner strength to overcome the challenge and bring the Ravioli back together. During these times great Ravioli managers don't resign, but continue the resolve, are Resilient and Recover to see that the Ravioli are made, and made even better.

RECOGNIZE, REWARD, REINFORCE AND REPEAT

Recognize, Reward, Reinforce and Repeat are important attributes to thank the Ravioli makers with consistent and exceptional efforts to keep the Ravioli dough going all day, every day. This Ravioli Rule is important because it improves morale, provides a mechanism to let the Ravioli makers know the managers appreciate the Ravioli being made the Right way and makes everyone part of the team.

Remember, you want to Recognize and Reward positive behavior so you Reinforce its importance and your Ravioli managers/makers Repeat the success. Use great Ravioli makers as good examples of the Ravioli model that other makers want to hold in high regard. It Reinforces all the Ravioli makers do the Right thing, follow the Ravioli models and emulate good behavior to make world class Ravioli.

A

ADAPTABLE

A is for being Adaptable. It is essential that the Ravioli manager/maker be Adaptable and flexible. It is being Adaptable to the process of making Ravioli, to the Ravioli makers, to the Ravioli machines and to the surprises that occur along the way. Sometimes, other events control the menu, and the ability to be Adaptable to changes in the menu is important to survive as a

Ravioli maker/manager. As Ravioli managers, you need to be Adaptable to the needs of the customer, which may differ from your perception of their needs.

Adaptability can also be assessed by moving Ravioli managers/makers to handle different responsibilities. If you are not willing to become Adaptable to changes, you will get burned when you drop the Ravioli in boiling water.

AGGREGATE

To be a great Ravioli manager/maker means you need to have more than one skill, more than one Ravioli rule to follow towards success. Therefore, it is essential you have an Aggregate set of skills and Ravioli Rules available to use. It is like being at a food buffet to pick the choice of food, experience all of them and then decide the one(s) you like and can use at the right time.

ACTION

Besides Adaptable and Aggregate, another one of the A set of skills you need to take is Action to get the job completed. Otherwise the Ravioli will never develop and it will just stay as bags of flour on the shelf and cartons of eggs sitting in the refrigerator. Action is more than just implementing the recipe; it is about having a sense of timeliness to get the job done.

ATTITUDE

Having a positive Attitude will make the difference in how you view making the Ravioli and how others view you. The positive Attitude helps when you need to respond to immediate and rapid changes—when you are Ready and Reliable—in the Ravioli environment. As leaders you should demonstrate the positive Attitude so people will be inspired by your behavior and know how to positively react to any situation.

ARTICULATE

Ravioli managers need to Articulate, to clearly, simply and concisely communicate the goals, directions and Ravioli Rules. It is about communicating meaningful information.

ATTENTION

Ravioli managers/makers need to pay Attention to their surroundings, to the detail of their work, to the people and the Ravioli machines to make sure the Ravioli are being made correctly.

ACCURACY

Make sure the Ravioli are made with Accuracy, which means the Ravioli are made with quality controls in place. The Accuracy rule ensures the Ravioli are made to the specifications described in the recipe, which leads to making high quality Ravioli. It means to execute flawlessly so the Ravioli customers have a quality experience.

ACUMEN

Ravioli managers need to have Acumen, which is the ability to understand and see what is not obvious to the average Ravioli maker. It is the ability to distinguish and choose what is right, true, correct, accurate, superficial, or excellent. It is having great perception into human behavior, and using good sound practical judgment.

AGILITY

Ravioli Managers/makers need to have Agility, which is basically a sense of urgency. It is being agile, nimble and quick, and makes the difference between you and other Ravioli Managers/Makers. It gives you the edge. You don't want to sacrifice any of the other rules for this rule. You need to balance the Agility rule with the other rules such as Accuracy and Attention.

AUTHENTIC

Being Authentic is essential to the overall relationship of great Ravioli managers/makers. Authentic is being genuine and real, it contributes to the motivation of all Ravioli managers/makers, leads to trust and believability. If you are not, everyone will know the difference. It is used in communicating with the top Ravioli chef, the person cleaning the machines, the person bringing in the supplies and the customer. Being Authentic leads to doing the Right thing.

V

VISION

V starts with a Vision, the foresight, the dream, the destination you want the Ravioli and Ravioli managers/makers to reach. You need to establish both long- and short-term Ravioli Vision plans. The Vision is a large-scale Ravioli menu-planning event and just as minor adjustments are made in the Ravioli recipe, you will need to make adjustments in the Vision as you are cooking to reach your destination.

VALUES

Values are the common bond that keeps the Ravioli and the Ravioli group together.

The Values are important because they are the basis for making sound decisions and exercising good judgment. Values provide a sense of personal belonging and the Ravioli team follows them as the commitment to making excellent Ravioli. Values set the highest standard of excellence, so that long after Alfredo and Mario have left the Ravioli business, the Ravioli managers/makers will know the reason why they are there for the Ravioli and will continue using the Values to successfully cook the Ravioli.

VARIETY

You need to have a Variety of experiences, whether you are moving from different Ravioli positions, self-educating, or learning from others. Variety of experiences rounds out Ravioli education, assists in shaping the future and contributes to personal and professional development.

VALUABLE

All Ravioli managers/makers/machines are Valuable and everyone, regardless of position, contributes to the Ravioli making process and should always be treated as being Valuable.

I

INTERPERSONAL RELATIONSHIPS

A critical and challenging rule is building strong Interpersonal Relationships with Ravioli owners, managers/makers and customers. Developing and strengthening these long-term relationships builds and continues to grow business and to get the Ravioli made. Using an Aggregate array of the Ravioli Rules sets the buffet table for starting, creating, developing and maintaining strong Interpersonal Relationships.

INTEGRITY

Integrity is a required Ravioli Rule for all managers/makers. It is key to developing trust, honesty and fairness among all customers and Ravioli makers. It builds team effort, assists in being Ready and Reliable, contributes towards Respect, increases morale, continues growth, supports strong

Interpersonal Relationships, promotes Open communication and adds credibility. It is great to have an impressive Reputation where people can count on you. Integrity, with or without it, means everything.

INTERDEPENDENCY

Interdependency creates the team. Just as the Ravioli Rules are interdependent, all Ravioli owners, managers and makers depend on each other and work together to operate as a strong team to achieve the Ravioli. One Ravioli maker is not as smart as ALL of the Ravioli makers.

Giving Ravioli managers/makers a Variety of experiences sharpens their Interdependent skills – it prevents them from thinking in silos, and allows them to view the entire team picture. A strong, Interdependent team fosters harmony, improves production, works well with one another and leads to success.

INNOVATION

I is for Innovation, which makes the difference between the generic Ravioli making companies and the great Ravioli making companies. Success is more than just about business as usual. The great Ravioli-making companies allow all managers/makers to be innovative and creative. Ravioli making companies that make the difference are Open to new ideas and Listen and Learn from the Innovative suggestions proposed by managers/makers.

O

OPEN

Ravioli owners/managers/makers create an Open environment where all sincerely Respect and care for each other, have a desire to understand each other, share Open and clear communications and information, and speak the truth. Ravioli managers/makers, as part of their responsibility, need to be Open and accessible to work with and Listen to Ravioli makers and customers.

OPPORTUNITY

Every Ravioli manager/maker should look at every Ravioli-making event—even the bad ones—as an Opportunity to make the best Ravioli. Improvement needs to be ongoing.

OWNERSHIP

All managers/makers own the Ravioli. They're entrusted with Ownership and process. They can't shirk the responsibilities; they view the process as if it is theirs alone and own it. It is an essential level of responsibility and maturity in the Ravioli making process.

OBJECTIVE

Objective has two different definitions for Ravioli managers/makers: First, it is the overriding goal and plan of Action that needs to be achieved to make the Ravioli. Second, you are managing fairly and not creating favorites in the Ravioli making operation.

OBSERVE

You learn by Observing – and that encompasses all facets of the process. Sometimes it is better to Observe, rather being the center of attention. This eliminates distraction and, in turn, increases focus. By Observing the best, you can learn from the best and improve. By Observing you can see the big picture and you can make sound decisions and take Action. Get out of the office. Walk around the place. Carefully watch the process. Observe the Ravioli.

L

LISTENING AND LEARNING

L is for Listening and Learning, which is one of the most underused Ravioli Rules. By truly Listening and Learning from people who know the most about the Ravioli process, you can rely upon their experience to learn, take Action and make the Right decision.

LEGACY

As Ravioli managers/makers, you should work hard and leave a World Class Legacy to your efforts and creativity. Set the highest standards. Create benchmarks in Ravioli history. Inspire other Ravioli makers/managers to do the same. They will carry on the Ravioli Legacy.

LEADER

You don't need to become the owner of a company to become a Leader. New Ravioli makers/managers are Leaders the moment they start learning how to make Ravioli and follow the rules.

LOGICAL

Ravioli managers/makers need to be Logical and think thoroughly about the process. They can't act on impulse or reaction. Being Logical is a complement to exercising good sound judgment and making Ravioli the right way.

LIKEABLE

Ravioli managers/makers in building their Interpersonal Relationships need to be Likeable. This applies in the delivery of good news and bad news.

LOYALTY

Loyalty to the Ravioli is paramount to organizational success. Be Loyal to the Ravioli and the Ravioli needs to be Loyal to you.

I

INCLUDE

Productivity and morale improves when you Include everyone in the process. All feel they are part of the team, someone special to the overall process. By Including, they all have an Opportunity to succeed.

INFORM

Inform all the Ravioli managers/makers about changes and improvements being made. Clearly Articulating and Informing them about what's cooking helps make them feel Included in the process.

INSPIRE

You need to continually Inspire all people to make the Ravioli, to get the most out of all their production deliverables and to reach the next level.

"Well, Gramps, that is it," the girls said simultaneously. "That's what we've learned from you, and that's what we offer. Alfredo looked at Mario, his eyes starting to mist. "What a wonderful gift."

Mario nodded and then looked at the girls. "We're glad we shared our story with you," he said. "It reaped so many additional rules. Thank you, girls! You learned well."

Both Grandfathers said, "Well what should we do now?" There was a brief pause, as each considered the question. Then they answered in unison: "Let's make some Ravioli!"

A Review

R stands for:
- Making Ravioli the Right Way.
- Respect the Ravioli
- Being Ready and Reliable
- Risk (Reputation)– mitigate it
- Reflection
- Resilience and Recovery, not Resignation
- Recognize, Reward, Reinforce and Repeat

A stands for:
- Adaptable.
- An Aggregate set of skills
- Action
- Attitude (positive!)
- Articulate
- Attention
- Accuracy
- Acumen
- Agility
- Authentic

V stands for:
- Vision
- Values
- Variety of experience
- Valuable

I stands for:
- Interpersonal Relationships
- Integrity
- Interdependency
- Innovation

O stands for:
- Open
- Opportunity
- Ownership
- Objective
- Observe

L stands for:
- Listening and Learning
- Legacy
- Leader
- Logical
- Likeable
- Loyalty

I stands for:
- Include
- Inform
- Inspire

Suggested Reading

A Passion for Excellence; The Leadership Difference--Tom Peters

Born to Win--Lewis Timberlake

Built to Last: Successful Habits of Visionary Companies--Jim Collins and Jerry I Porras

Cigars, Whiskey and Winning: Leadership Lessons from General Ulysses S. Grant-- Al Kaltman

Creativity: How Leaders Gain or Lose it, Why People Demand It --James M. Krouzes and Barry Posner

First Break All the Rules: What the Worlds Greatest Managers Do Differently --Marcus Buckingham and Curt Coffman

Fish A Remarkable Way to Boost Morale and Improve Results--Stephen Lundin; Harry Paul; John Christensen, Ken Blanchard

Get Everyone in your Boat Rowing in the same Direction: 5 Leadership Principals to Follow So Others Will Follow You--Bob Boylan

Good to Great: Why Some Companies Make the Leap... and Others Don't--James Collins

Gung Ho! Turning on the People in any Organization--Kenneth Blanchard and Sheldon Bowles

High Five the Magic of Working Together --Ken Blanchard, Sheldon Bowles Don Care and Eunice-Parisi-Carew

In Search of Excellence: Lessons from Americas Best Run Companies--Robert H Waterman Thomas J Peters

It's Always Too Soon to Quit-- Lewis Timberlake

Lincoln on Leadership: Executive Strategies for Tough Times-- Donald T. Phillips

Joe Torre's Ground Rules for Winners--Joe Torre with Henry Dreher

Leadership Mastery: How to Challenge Yourself and Others to Greatness--Dale Carnegie

Leadership Secrets of Attila the Hun--Wess Roberts

Listen for Success: A Guide to Effective Listening-- A Robertson

Management by Baseball--Jeff Angus

Remember This Titan: The Bill Yoast Story : Lessons Learned From A Celebrated Coach's Journey As Told to Steve Sullivan

The Customer Driven Company Moving from Talk to Action--Richard C Whitely

The Flexible Thinker--Michael Rosenberg

The Loyalty Effect--Frederick Reichfield

The Power of Nice: How to Negotiate So Everyone Wins – Especially You!-- Ronald M. Shapiro and Mark A Jankowski with James Dale

The Seven Habits of Highly Effective People-- Stephen R Covey

Who Moved My Cheese --Spencer Johnson

Winning Through Innovation--Michael I Tushman and Charles A. O'Reilly II

Zapp!! The Lightning of Empowerment--William C. Byham

The Recipes

So as I sent a draft of my book to some friends for review, they suggested adding a Ravioli recipe to the book. At first I wasn't supportive of the idea since a recipe didn't fit into the management book. However, the suggestion became more common, from people located in different areas of the country, having never met and I am their only common connection.

To assist in my decision, I used the Ravioli Rules to be Open to an Innovative idea. So after Reflecting and Listening to several friends I decided to take Action and add a Ravioli Recipe. Then, after some additional Reflection and to be even more Innovative I decided to add more that just a Ravioli Recipe.

So I actually have 2 recipes for you.

A traditional Ravioli Recipe that can also be used as any pasta recipe, such as linguine, fettuccine, pappardelle. But for our purposes here it is a Ravioli Recipe.

There are a variety of Ravioli recipes. There are so many variations with semolina flour, white flour, eggs and additional egg yolks, egg yolks only. We can write a book just on the variations of Ravioli dough and the appropriate stuffing. I am just using a basic Ravioli pasta dough recipe.

The second pasta recipe is for Cavatelli. These are homemade pasta I would have as a young boy. It is a simple recipe my mom made with flour and water.

The real bonuses in this section are the homemade tomato sauce recipes. I decided to share.

Basic Ravioli Pasta Dough

2 Cups (about) soft wheat flour (any white flour will do and I am not endorsing any brands, but King Arthur and White Lily are good versions to use)

3 Large eggs

1/4 to1/2 teaspoon salt (optional)

First Step--Start the Dough

Place flour in a food processor or mixer with dough hooks. Add eggs.

Food processor: pulse until clumps of moist dough form (do not process into ball).

Mixer: use the dough hooks to knead the dough into a slight ball shape.

You will still use hands to knead the dough.

Work the dough on a lightly floured work surface and shape it into ball. Knead the dough mixture until smooth, add a slight dusting of flour if it is sticking. The hand kneading process should take about 5 minutes. Wrap it in plastic, or a plastic bag with a little flour, and let it rest at room temperature from 30 minutes to 2 hours.

At this point you can have a glass of wine and/or start making the Ravioli filling and then you can roll the dough.

Roll the dough using a Pasta Machine--Roll the dough into sheets

Cut the dough into about 6-8 equal pieces. Cover them with plastic wrap, a towel, or keep them in the plastic bag to keep the dough from drying out. Set the pasta machine to the widest setting so you can incrementally flatten the dough to the right thickness. Flatten 1 dough piece at a time into a rectangle and roll it through the pasta machine. Keep folding it in half and rolling it through the pasta machine, alternating the ends as you roll the dough through the pasta machine.

You need to keep rolling the pasta dough, reducing the machine settings and lightly sprinkling the dough with flour to keep the pasta from sticking, until the pasta sheet is about 12-16 inches long. It needs to be about 1/16 inch thick--although you can adjust the width for a thicker dough and length for a shorter dough. Place the pasta sheet on lightly floured work surface; cover with a towel or plastic. Repeat the process with the remaining pasta sheets.

When your Ravioli filling is ready, lay out the sheets one at a time and line them up side by side, but not on top of each other. One sheet is for the bottom layer and the filling will be placed on this pasta sheet. The alternate sheet will form the top after the filling is applied. You can decide how large you want the Ravioli, but you should be able to get about 2 Ravioli across the width. It should measure about 1 ½ to 2 inch squares, unless you want a larger size Ravioli. Using two spoons, place about a tablespoon of filling into each estimated square. When you have completed the placing of the filling on the pasta sheet lightly brush one egg beaten with 1 tablespoon of water and brush up and down the sheet alongside the filling. This will form a seal when the second pasta sheet is applied. Place the second pasta sheet over the first sheet and press down around the filling areas to form a little dome or pocket and press down around the domes and the edges of the pasta sheets to make sure they all sealed. Cut the pasta with either a cookie/pastry wheel to form fluted edges or a pizza cutter for a straight cut.

Place the Ravioli on parchment paper or wood boards and cover with a towel or plastic wrap. Don't place the Ravioli on each other; they need some distance so they will not stick. You can lightly sprinkle the board with flour to keep the Ravioli from sticking. At this point you are ready to cook or freeze the Ravioli. They cook in rapid boiling water for about 3-4 minutes. Keep a careful watch. When they reach the top of the boiling water they are ready. Taste test one to see if they are ready.

Roll the Dough using a hand roller.

If you do not have a pasta maker, you can roll out the dough by hand with a wooden rolling pin. This is the old fashioned way. So you can roll out the dough either all of it or half at a time to the same thickness as described above. At this point, you would apply the stuffing by using the portion of the dough on your far left to use as the top sheet of the Ravioli. So you would start applying the stuffing about 4-5 inches in from the far left of the dough, in the same proportion as you would in the pasta sheets above. About 1 ½ to 2 inch squares, 2 columns of stuffing, unless you want a larger Ravioli. When you have completed placing the stuffing, brush the water or egg water mixture on the dough by the stuffing to keep the seal tight. Pick up the dough on the far left side and drape it over the side with the stuffing. Press down around the stuffing areas to form a little dome or pocket to make sure they all sealed. Cut the pasta with either a cookie/pastry wheel to form fluted edges or a pizza cutter for a straight cut.

Other Innovative Ravioli

You can add your own signature Ravioli and make changes to add flavor to the dough by adding tomato paste, pesto sauce, chopped green basil or spinach. A variation I thought was using Chesapeake Bay Seasoning to the dough and adding crabmeat into the filling mix. Let your Innovative mind work to create your own signature Ravioli.

Easy Ravioli Filling/Stuffing:

    1 Pound of Ricotta Cheese
    1 egg for every pound of Ricotta
    ½ cup to 1 cup of Romano Cheese
    ½ cup to 1 cup of Mozzarella Cheese (or a four cheese Italian Blend)
    ¼ to ½ of cup of Parsley
Mix all of the above together.

Cavatelli or Handmade Pasta

2 cups or more of the soft wheat flour as described above.
1 cup of hot water divided in half (using hot water makes a lighter Cavatelli)

This pasta can be made with a food processor or dough hooks, but I like the old fashioned way of making this strictly as handmade pasta. Place 2 cups flour in a large bowl or on a wooden board making a well in center. Gradually add the 1/2 cup hot water, a touch of salt to the flour and stir the mixture to combine. Slowly mix the flour with the water and then add the remaining water to form a soft dough. If you are making the dough on the board be careful to gradually pull the flour into the water well, to mix the ingredients carefully and avoid a water break of the flour wall. Using a wooden board that has been lightly floured, place the dough on the board and knead with your hands until smooth. If the dough is sticky, simply add more flour to make a smooth dough. This process should take about 5 minutes. Roll the dough into a ball and transfer it to a lightly floured bowl and cover it with plastic wrap. Or you can place it in a lightly floured food storage bag and let it rest at room temperature for 1-2 hours, while you make sauce and have a glass of wine.

Lightly dust the wooden board with flour, put the dough on the board and cut off about a 1 inch-thick slice. Start to roll the dough between the palms of the hands and on the lightly floured board to about a 1/3-inch-thick rope, like a long pretzel rod. Repeat this step with equal parts of the dough slices, rolling each into rope. Cut the ropes into 1-inch lengths or about the size of a small pretzel nugget. Now you need to roll them into the handmade cavatelli shape. Using the longer side of your thumb, horizontal to the work surface, take each small nugget sized dough and starting at one end, press on it and push your thumb on the dough away from you until the dough is free from your thumb. You should have horizontal imprints on the dough and it should be curved.

Keep the cavatelli separated from the working area of the wooden board if it is large enough, or transfer the cavatelli to a baking sheet lightly floured. Repeat this process with the remaining dough.. They can be made a few hours ahead. Cover them with a dry kitchen towel and let them stay at room temperature.

Bring a large pot of salted water to a boil. Add the cavatelli and boil them until tender, but still firm to bite(al dente), usually less than 30 seconds after they rise to the top of the boiling water. The best way to know if they are done is to taste them – remember tender but slightly firm to the bite. Drain well; return to the pot or place in a dish with the sauce.

The Tomato Sauce(Gravy)

While I hope the largest portion of this book has served to improve and sharpen your management skills, this next recipe for success will change your sauce for pasta. These two recipes are ones that my family has used for years. The first recipe is made with meat and is called gravy and it can be used with Ravioli, of course, and Spaghetti, Manicotti, Lasagna...basically any pasta. The second one is a meatless sauce that is made with garlic and called marinara, usually used with a linguine, fettuccine or spaghetti...again, any pasta and maybe you would serve it with a fish or chicken dish.

The challenge I had in writing both of these sauces is the recipes have been held by memory, using experience and the senses of touch, smell, taste and feel.

So I have done my best to taste and test the sauces. I want to do what is Right and be clear and precise in Articulating the directions, so the gravy/sauce is Likeable and you will be Inspired to use this new recipe for your pasta as your new Legacy sauce.

Before we begin, I should start by first telling you the ingredient you should not use. The secret is DO NOT USE a tomato sauce product that contains sugar, corn syrup, fructose syrup and DO NOT UNDER ANY circumstance add sugar to the recipe.

Gravy

3 large cans of tomato sauce (29 oz size) (remember note above)

2 cans of tomato paste (8 oz size)

½ to 1 teaspoon of salt

½ to 1 teaspoon of pepper

½ to 1 teaspoon of garlic powder

(As you gain experience making your sauce you can add more or less of spice to suit your taste.)

Add the sauce, paste and seasonings to a large pot on medium heat and stir all the ingredients.

Meatballs (Made in advance)

Add the meatballs. (Made Ahead)

2 pounds of ground beef

½ teaspoon of salt (not kosher salt)

¼ -½ teaspoon of black pepper

½ teaspoon of garlic powder

½ to 1 teaspoon of minced onions

¼ cup Parsley flakes

1/3 cup Italian flavored bread crumbs

1/3 cup Romano Cheese

1/3 cup milk

2 eggs (1 egg for every pound of meat)

Mix all the ingredients. I first use a large serving fork, but then use my hands to complete the mixing process. I prefer mixing them by hand rather than a mixer with dough hooks to maintain the homemade texture of the meatball. Shape the meat into meatballs and start frying in a saucepan with a little oil just covering the pan so the meatballs don't stick when you first start to fry them. Fry the meatballs turning each side as they brown. Drain them on a paper towel to absorb the oil.

(Also for clarity you can alter the volume of some of the dry seasonings above based on your taste. If you want more or less garlic powder, onions etc.)

Sausage

Fry up about 8 large sweet Italian sausage links until brown on each side and drain on a paper towel.

The Gravy

While the sauce is starting to heat add the meatballs and sausage and let the sauce boil. When it reaches the boiling point lower the heat to let it simmer. Remember to use a wooden spoon and stir the bottom of the sauce pot to prevent it from burning, which happens frequently on electric stoves, or if you have used thick puree, crushed tomatoes and the sauce is very thick.

Let the sauce simmer for about 45 minutes and stirring the bottom about every 5 minutes so it doesn't stick and burn.

The real bonus that adds additional sweetness to the sauce is to also add one or two fried spareribs and fried pork chops at the same time you add the fried meatballs and sausage to the sauce. Finally, in the last five to ten minutes of the sauce cooking add about 5-8 large fresh basil leaves to the sauce. You can either add them whole or just add them chopped to the sauce. The fresh basil imparts a nice flavor to the sauce. You are ready to serve your sauce with your cooked pasta. I like to serve the meat separate from the pasta.

Marinara Sauce

1 large can of tomato sauce (29 oz)--remember the note above

1 can tomato sauce (8 oz)

1 can of tomato paste (8 oz)

½ to 1 teaspoon of salt

½ to 1 teaspoon of garlic powder or about 4 fresh garlic cloves peeled and sliced or chopped.

1 teaspoon of Oregano or Italian Seasoning.

¼ - 1/3 cup virgin olive oil

This is a simple 30-minute tomato sauce that is used over spaghetti, linguine, almost any pasta even Ravioli, maybe except for lasagna.

Heat up about a ¼ to 1/3 cup of virgin olive oil add the fresh garlic. You need to let the garlic get tan, but not burn over a medium to high heat and you can smell the aroma of the garlic. The critical moment is when the oil is hot enough that you hear a sizzle and steam sound when you add the 8 oz canned tomato sauce. To reach this temperature you should wait about 5 minutes or less after you turn on the heat. It is when the garlic is tan and not browned and you can smell the aroma of the garlic. (You may just have to practice to get it right). If you use garlic powder or dehydrated garlic instead of fresh garlic cloves, the time frame is reduced since this ingredient burns quickly.

Once the sizzle and steam sound is complete, you add the remaining tomato sauce, paste and dry ingredients. Once it reaches a boil, keep it over a medium heat to simmer and keep stirring the sauce every 5 minutes to keep it from sticking to the bottom of the pot. (After experience you can add more or less garlic or oregano to suit your taste) If you want you can add fresh basil in the last 5 minutes of cooking. This process should take 30 minutes and you are ready to serve your sauce.

Variation: Instead of garlic you can omit the garlic and make a very sweet sauce using about 1 medium onion and sautéing it in olive oil. You don't need to hear the sizzle and steam sound for this sauce. All the other ingredients stay the same. But the garlic marinara is the best.

Buon Appetito!

About the Author

The author started his career as an intern in the Pennsylvania General Assembly while a graduate student at the Pennsylvania State University. He served as Director of the House of Representatives Policy Committee and Senior Research Analyst for the House Insurance Committee. He was Legislative Director for the Pennsylvania Insurance Commissioner where he managed the legislative strategy leading to the enactment of 37 insurance laws over an eight-year period and the Senate confirmation of 2 Insurance Commissioners. The cornerstone of the administration was the enactment of the Governor's Auto Insurance Reform Proposal (Act 6 of 1990), saving Pennsylvania consumers $1 billion in its first 5 years.

He was employed with MBNA America in a series of progressive management experiences. Initially, he was selected as a member of the management team in establishing an auto insurance program for MBNA(a major cross sell initiative) – based on his strong customer service expertise and auto insurance industry knowledge. He served as the first Delaware licensed property and casualty insurance agent and as a Marketing Manager/Account Executive in the Insurance business. Given his expertise in working with diverse and often challenging constituencies, Al was asked to take a leadership role in Quality Assurance. He worked in the highly respected Quality Assurance business area managing 3 of the 4 business areas. Here he managed Customer communications with Executives, the company's innovation program, and the enterprisewide daily matrix and incentive program on Customer Satisfaction, which was featured in a 1996 Fortune magazine article. After the purchase by Bank of America, Al worked as Operations Manager, Executive Relations in the Chairman's Office handling Customer relationships. In 2006, Al's work was recognized with Bank of America Card Services Award of Excellence.

Al is now currently employed for a non-profit in Delaware where he managed the distribution of over $2 million of funding in less than one year for the statewide Crisis Alleviation program.

The author graduated from St. Raymond's High School in the Bronx, Iona College with a degree in Political Science and a Master's Degree in Public Administration from the Pennsylvania State University.